# LIVING SMALL

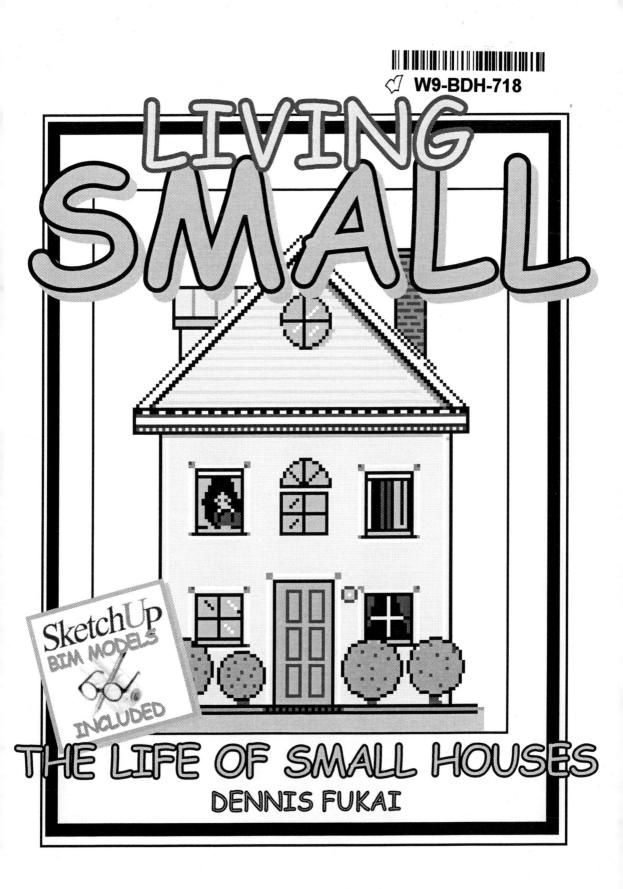

SketchUp
BIM MODELS
INCLUDED

# THE LIFE OF SMALL HOUSES

## DENNIS FUKAI

a publication of

I n s i t e b u i l d e r s . c o m
16708 SW 132nd Lane
Archer FL 32618
(352) 870-9357

dennis@insitebuilders.com

## ACKNOWLEDGEMENTS

Thanks again to @Last Sofware, Inc. and its founder Brad Schell for their continued support and commitment to three dimensional construction communications.

Also thanks to Rick Thompson, Jay Shafer, Greg Johnson, and squatters Amelia and Victor for use of their design and construction information.

Special thanks to Patrick Scoggin, Phillip Meadow, Steve Johnson, David Terry, Bryce Stout, Todd Burch, Kevin Rowell, Alan Fraser, and the many other experts who lend their time and talent to the SketchUp Users Forum http://sketchup.com/forum.

And finally, thanks to Barbara Fukai, the editor, coordinator, marketer and publisher who made this book physically possible.

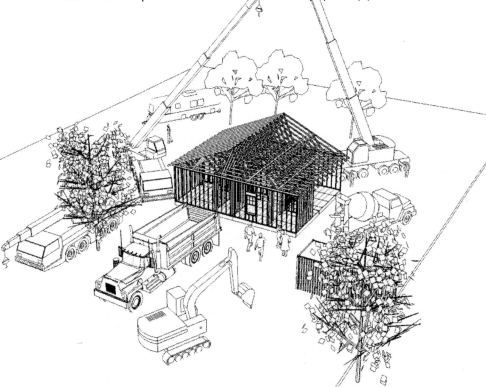

## GLOSSARY of some terms:

Architectural model: used to study style, vernacular, or aesthetic features of a building.
Balloon framing: a framing method where the walls extend from foundation to roof.
Bandbox: very small multi-story townhouses built in high density neighborhoods.
Building Information Model: a three-dimensional construction information model.
Bungalow: a single story house with low sloping roofs, a veranda, and an occupied attic.
Camelback: a shotgun house with a stair added to the front room to bedrooms above.
Cantilever: a projection or alcove that projects beyond a structural support like a foundation.
Chickee: the thatched house built by the Seminole people that inspired the Crackers.
Clerestory: a high window set into the roof line of a building for ventilation and light.
Construction model: includes structure, framing, finish and system details of a building.
Convection: heat transfer that occurs with the movement of air from one area to another.
Crackers: self-sufficient men and women who built homes and settled the southern USA.
Crawl space: area under a house big enough for someone to access and service a building.
Dog trot: an open breezeway in a cracker house that evolved into an enclosed hall.
Double-pen: a cracker house with two rooms and two fireplaces.
Extruded floor plan: a two dimensional house plan and rooms with flat ceilings.
Fly-by: an animation technique used to view a 3D model from above.
Four square: a cracker style house with broad porches and steeply pitched roofs.
Frontier settlers: settlers who built homes on the frontiers of newly occupied land.
Gate piers: vertical structures that flank an entry to a building site.
Heavy timber: a framing method that uses heavy wood members and non-bearing walls.
HVAC: heating, ventilation, and air conditioning equipment and associated duct work.
I-House: a cracker house with a stair from a dog-trot to bedrooms on a second floor.
Life Cycle: the service life of a material, fixture, equipment, or furnishing of a building.
McMansion: a large house produced to sell in a competitive consumer market.
Mini-McMansion: a smaller version of a McMansion that can be sold at a lower cost.
Mud and waddle: construction that uses mud packed into a wood lattice to create a wall.
Need: a necessity or absolute must critical to the function of a building.
Pioneers: men, women, and children who settled the wilderness as frontier settlers.
Platform framing: a framing method where the framed walls extend from floor to floor.
Purlins: horizontal structural members that transfer roof loads to the roof beams.
Purposeful: showing a clear determination with a definite purpose or aim.
Resources: includes available labor and materials like sand, stones, trees, and water.
Ridge: the horizontal line formed by the upper edges of two sloping roofs.
Saddlebag: a cracker house with two rooms and a fireplace in the wall between the rooms.
Sappy trees: wood like pine and cedar that have natural oils used for roof shingles.
Seminoles: a Native American society that escaped to present day Florida.
Shoji Screen: a light weight, semi-transparent wood frame and paper wall panel.
Shotgun house: a long and narrow house with rooms directly in line with each other.
Sidehall house: a shotgun with a side porch or corridor that allowed access to rear rooms.
Slums: neighborhoods with poorly maintained and deteriorating housing.
Stock lumber sizes: standard framing members that facilitate construction planning.
Tract homes: mass-produced houses with similar style and floor plans by one builder.
Truss: a structural element made up of a combination of members in a triangular arrangement.
USA: United States of America used to illustrate typical patterns of development.
Vernacular: an indigenous building style using local materials and traditional methods.
Walk-through: an animation technique used to view a 3D model from eye level.
Want: a desire or wish not necessarily critical to the function of a building.

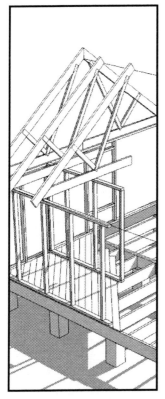

*Dennis Fukai is a licensed architect and construction manager with more than thirty years experience as a professional construction administrator, researcher, and university professor. He is a Fulbright Scholar and earned his PhD in architecture from the University of California, Berkeley. Dennis is dedicated to the design and construction of small houses and has been recognized internationally for his work with construction modeling, building information modeling, and graphic communications.*

# INTRODUCTION
## Overview

Mass produced houses are built to meet the demands of a general housing market. Small houses are built purposefully with clearly defined functions in mind. This sense of specific purpose gives the spaces inside and outside a small house its shape and form.

In its earliest form, the result was a simple and sustainable shelter. However, even the crudest shelters only succeeded when builders could define the fundamental purpose and basic needs required of their house. These needs were governed by an understanding of the environment and community that surrounded the house. This sense of community included contact with neighbors, resources, work, and those that brought meaning to an often difficult life.

Once the intent was clear, small houses combined inside and outside spaces to support activities beyond the walls of the house. This can be seen in the porches and living areas of the simplest settler's shelter. Interior and exterior spaces worked together to support the work necessary for survival.

Manufactured materials standardized construction and made a settler's house more comfortable, but it was the simplicity of these small houses that helped focus attention on the work at hand.

As such, small houses were built to support functional needs. For example, rooms were added to the house with doors that opened directly to activity areas on a farm or ranch. This included porches, naturally shaded areas, fields, and outbuildings that were integral parts of these small houses.

Small houses later filled the need for basic housing. Here the purpose of the house shifted to the need for efficient homes that could support the people working on farms and in factories.

The efficiency of these houses was shaped by the standard construction methods and materials that emerged from a growing demand for housing.

With increasing demand, worker housing evolved into an even greater need for affordable housing. This began in some cities with townhouses built in high density neighborhoods adjacent to the work. Many of these compact buildings quickly deteriorated into slums because they could not adapt to the changing needs of their residents.

Flexible housing solutions were found in small houses that adjusted to the changing needs of their owners. This included adding stylized features and details that allowed small houses to be personalized with landscaping, decoration, and a parking space for the family car.

In the end, the purposeful nature of small houses can be summarized in the emerging counter-culture of very small houses. Tiny houses return to the clear purpose and fundamental needs of simple sustainable shelter. As such, even the smallest house can be comfortable if it includes a blend of multipurpose interior and exterior spaces.

The size and mobility of a tiny house reduces its impact on the environment and most importantly remains flexible, even deconstructible, so that it can take advantage of new materials and technologies as the house evolves and changes over time.

Be sure to view the 3D models for each of these houses on the CD as you read the book.

# CHAPTER ONE
## Living LARGE

MASS PRODUCED HOUSES ARE BUILT TO SELL TO A GENERAL MARKET

Living small means editing ones life to live simply, cutting the clutter and losing the weight of consumption. Living large means having whatever you want whenever you need it.

### McMansions
People who live large, need big houses where they can relax and feel good about what they've accomplished. Big houses have rooms that separate functions into compartments. These compartments organize the possessions of a large life into arrangements that represent the things that are important to living a large life.

Volumes of space are vital to living a large life. Extra space increases the perspective and extravagance that is the reward for living large. Ongoing success makes it important to continually expand an already large house or super-size a new house to fit ever increasing wants and desires.

The cost of maintaining a large life is only one of many challenges for people living large, but cost is an insignificant expense when weighed against the comfort found in the values of a big house.

### MiniMcMansions
Many people are forced to live uncomfortably in houses that do not fit their possessions. In these houses, wants and needs tend to overflow and unfulfilled needs no longer fit into otherwise large lifestyles.

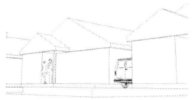

This means many people have a tough time fitting into small spaces. In fact, squeezing a lot of possessions into a small house only leads to frustration and general dissatisfaction with their home. This makes it very difficult for some people to relax and be comfortable in a small house. The only recourse is to work harder and make more money to buy a bigger house.

## A McMansion is a big house*

The **design** and construction of a McMansion **follows** a typical market driven **formula** that includes a set of all the standard **sales** features that make them appealing to potential **homebuyers.**

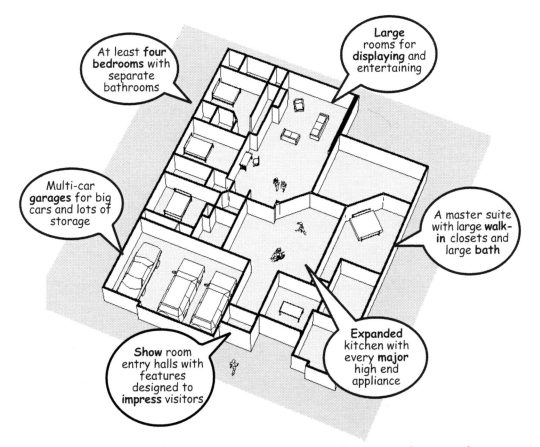

At least **four bedrooms** with separate bathrooms

**Large** rooms for **displaying** and entertaining

Multi-car **garages** for big cars and lots of storage

A master suite with large **walk-in** closets and large **bath**

**Show** room entry halls with features designed to **impress** visitors

Expanded kitchen with every **major** high end appliance

Developers of McMansions must **always** include an assortment of **eye catching** materials and options that increase **marketability** and the final **sales** price.

### In the kitchen:

Stone or faux stone countertops
A prep island with sink and cooktop
Simulated wood or tile floors
Laminated wood cabinets
Two door refrigerators
Chef style stainless ranges
Double ovens and microwaves
Informal eating areas with stools

### In the master bedroom:

Double sink and countertops
Toilet compartment
Over size bath tub
Separate glass enclosed shower
Triple size closets
Jewelry drawers
Marble, granite, and stone tile
Precious metal fixtures

*Also known as estate homes, beltway baronials, starter castles, off-the-rack, and themed houses

McMansions are designed to **appeal** to home **buyers** who want or need a large house to **entertain** friends and family and **display** their many possessions.

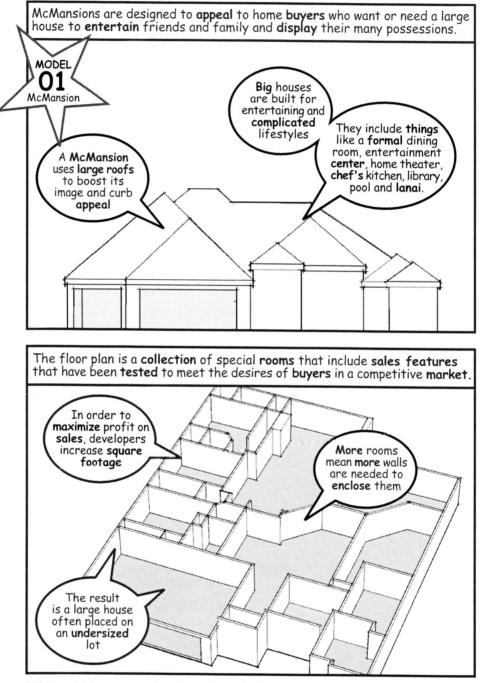

MODEL
**01**
McMansion

A **McMansion** uses **large roofs** to boost its image and curb **appeal**

**Big** houses are built for entertaining and **complicated** lifestyles

They include **things** like a **formal** dining room, entertainment **center**, home theater, **chef's** kitchen, library, pool and **lanai**.

The floor plan is a **collection** of special **rooms** that include **sales features** that have been **tested** to meet the desires of **buyers** in a competitive **market**.

In order to **maximize** profit on **sales**, developers increase **square footage**

More rooms mean **more** walls are needed to **enclose** them

The result is a large house often placed on an **undersized** lot

*This model is one of the top sellers of a major residential developer in the USA

The result is an **inefficient house** with the luxury of little used space for the sake of **extra** square footage that **consumes** energy, time, and resources.

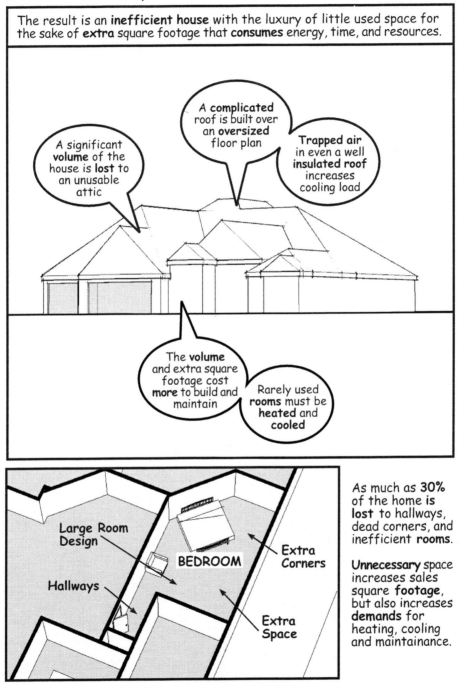

As much as **30%** of the home **is lost** to hallways, dead corners, and inefficient **rooms**.

**Unnecessary** space increases sales square **footage**, but also increases **demands** for heating, cooling and maintainance.

11

Resources consumed for construction*

Large **housing** developments **consume land** and other natural **resources**.

Millions of **tons of resources** are used in the construction of a **McMansion**

**More** than six hundred **trees** must be **cut** for the average McMansion.

Roof Trusses

Wall framing

As much as **50%** of the **trees** are nailed together to enclose **unusable** space

The ongoing **challenge** of all McMansions is that they **require** even more **resources** and maintenance to **keep** them **comfortable** for their owners.

In the **summer** attic temperatures rise **well above** the outside air

In the **winter** the same space becomes **cold soaked**

Thousands of **BTUs** and **barrels** of oil are embedded in the **roofing** on a McMansion

1000's of gallons of fertilizer, fuel, **insecticide**, and **water** are required to **maintain** a McMansion

*See "Sourcebook for Green and Sustainable Construction" at www.greenbuilder.com

Mini McMansions are **built** to appeal to home buyers looking for a **less** expensive house with as many of the **same** market **features** as possible.

Built for **entertainment** and display but **not** for simple living

**McMansion**

Mini McMansions take a **smaller** less expensive approach to a middle market

The **same** waste and **inefficiency** are included

**Mini McMansion**

MODEL **02** MiniMc

Inefficient space remains in smaller **rooms**

The same **rooms** are **squeezed** into less square **footage**

**Lower** cost often means **materials** with shorter lifecycles

## Mini McMansions squeeze in the sales features

The smaller size of a **Mini McMansion** reduces cost and **consumption** but the house often remains **inefficient** and expensive to maintain.

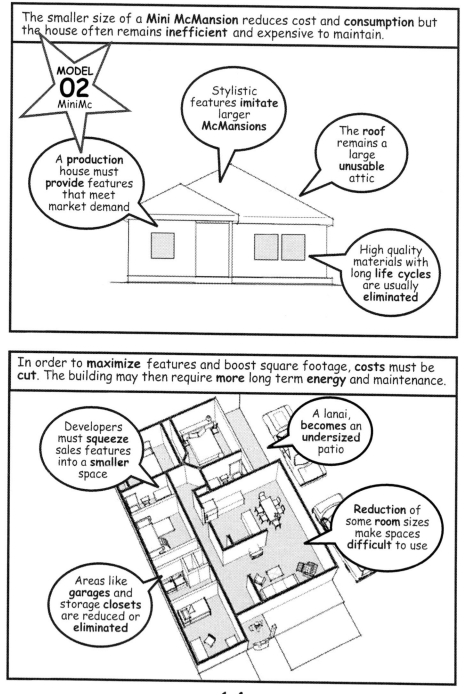

MODEL **02** MiniMc

Stylistic features **imitate** larger **McMansions**

The **roof** remains a large **unusable** attic

A **production** house must **provide** features that meet market demand

High quality materials with long **life cycles** are usually **eliminated**

In order to **maximize** features and boost square footage, **costs** must be **cut**. The building may then require **more** long term **energy** and maintenance.

Developers must **squeeze** sales features into a **smaller** space

A lanai, **becomes** an **undersized** patio

Reduction of some **room** sizes make spaces **difficult** to use

Areas like **garages** and storage **closets** are reduced or **eliminated**

## Common Sales Features

Developments that are nostagically named for the things that have been lost to build them

Market driven landscapes that enhance the "decorated box"

Streets lined with similar or identical houses equalize the homeowners in a neighborhood

Restrictive covenants that enforce unity and conformity to protect values

Minimum square footage requirements to keep out smaller homes or rental families

An elaborate sign or gate piers identify the community even if there is no gate

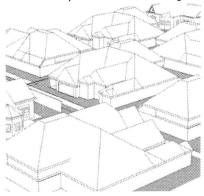

High density is necessary to amortize amenities and maximize returns

Market demand and high land cost often make the houses too big for their lots

### House design features
Stylistic decoration applied to the house to differentiate similar models

A tall and complex roof that gives the house curb appeal

At least one cupola, dormer, pediment, Palladian or oculus (round) window

Double wide or oversized single entry doors with decorated glass sidelights

Two story entry halls with staircases that open to upper floors

Dramatic lighting washes walls, rooms, shelves and countertops

A collection of separate and private rooms connected by corridors

An entry porch designed for display and decoration

Lots of floor space used for corridors with extra alcoves for displays

Master suites with separate closets, toilets, showers, and large spa tub

Recreation and theater rooms used only on special occasions

A garage big enough for two cars and bikes, boats, carts, and lots of stuff

### Sized for sales
Designed after careful market research in order to sell the most popular features

Must give the impression of size, whether spacious inside or not

Sales value and financing are based on size and room count

Design details applied to the house to meet customer demand

Complex electronics gadgets for security, entertainment, networking, and controls

Furnished sales models that would be impractical to duplicate in a real home

# CHAPTER TWO

## Living SMALL

Living small is difficult because no one is selling small. There are no sales options, no features to chose. To live small one has to be self determined and understand the motions and activities that make up the fundamentals of ones life.

This starts with needing less simply because there are no extras to want. Living small means functions and intents are clearly defined. Life has been scaled to the fundamentals necessary to support the essentials of a simple way of living.

### Purposeful
A well defined life also means a person is able to take a carefully considered approach to what goes into his or her home. This means the house is shaped by a well understood collection of needs.

A small house embodies this well defined way of living. A small house must be purposeful. The shape of a small house reflects the needs that exist within the lifestyle that it supports.

### Granny house
This idea of function and purpose can be seen in a "granny" house built as an assisted care dwelling unit. This small house was built to provide long-term comfort and care in an accessible and independent setting. It uses its interior to create a space to stimulate and excite the imagination.

### Family house
A small family house must have this same clear intent. There is order to a small house simply because its builder had an understanding of the absolute needs required for its purpose. This can be seen in the well crafted home built to meet the needs of a young family living in a complex world.

The lifestyle of the family remains clearly defined within spaces that fit the activities of their lives. The house converts square footage into an assortment of spaces that can change and blend into cross functions and multiple purposes.

### Efficient houses fulfill well defined needs*

Identifying **function** and **purpose** in a small house means listing the fundamental **needs** that must be met as a clearly **defined** set of preferences and **priorities**.

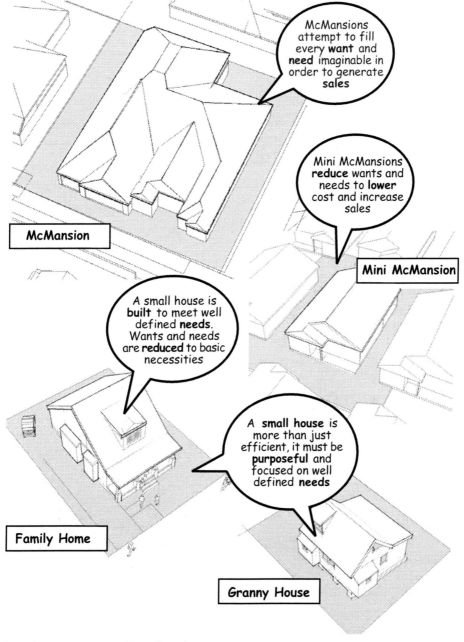

McMansions attempt to fill every **want** and **need** imaginable in order to generate **sales**

Mini McMansions **reduce** wants and needs to **lower** cost and increase sales

**McMansion**

**Mini McMansion**

A small house is **built** to meet well defined **needs**. Wants and needs are **reduced** to basic necessities

A **small house** is more than just efficient, it must be **purposeful** and focused on well defined **needs**

**Family Home**

**Granny House**

*Needs are necessities, things that a house must have to be a home

Life must be simple to live in a small house

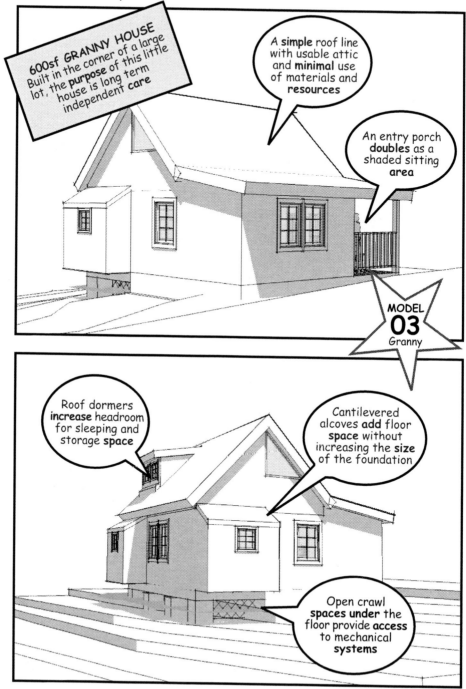

600sf GRANNY HOUSE
Built in the corner of a large lot, the **purpose** of this little house is long term independent **care**

A **simple** roof line with usable attic and **minimal** use of materials and **resources**

An entry porch **doubles** as a shaded sitting **area**

MODEL
**03**
Granny

Roof dormers **increase** headroom for sleeping and storage **space**

Cantilevered alcoves **add** floor **space** without increasing the **size** of the foundation

Open crawl **spaces under** the floor provide **access** to mechanical **systems**

# Basic needs filled by multipurpose rooms

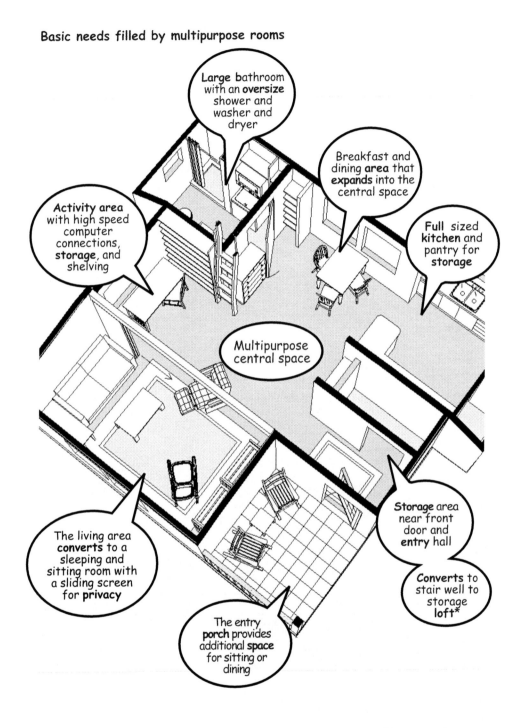

Large bathroom with an **oversize** shower and washer and dryer

Breakfast and dining **area** that **expands** into the central space

**Activity area** with high speed computer connections, **storage**, and shelving

Full sized **kitchen** and pantry for **storage**

Multipurpose central space

The living area **converts** to a sleeping and sitting room with a sliding screen for **privacy**

Storage area near front door and **entry** hall

**Converts** to stair well to storage **loft***

The entry **porch** provides additional **space** for sitting or dining

19 *The ability for a small house to adapt over time is a key to its efficiency

A small house must be open and imaginative

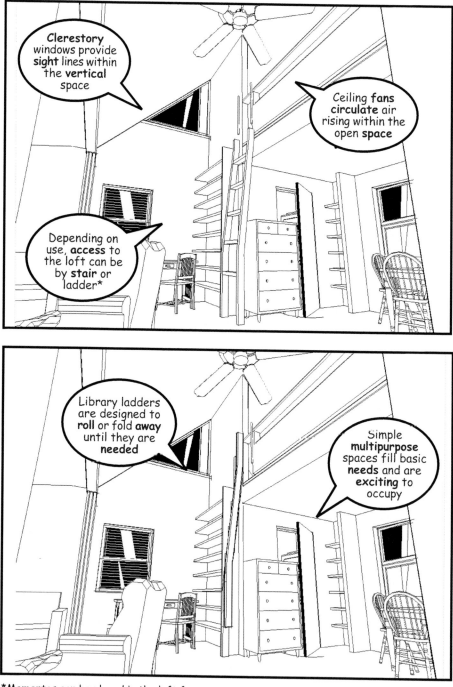

*Momentos can be placed in the loft for long-term storage by care givers

## A loft organizes the house three dimensionally

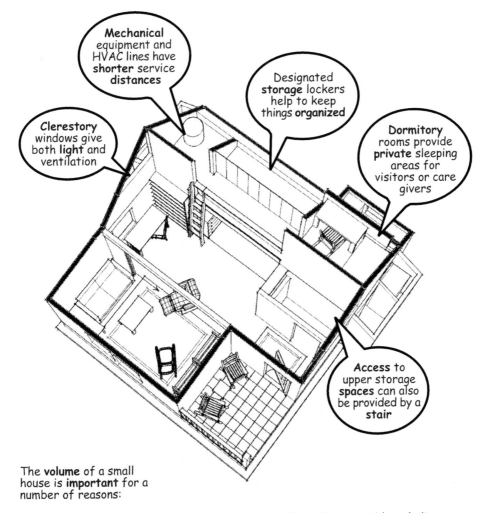

**Mechanical** equipment and HVAC lines have **shorter** service distances

Designated **storage** lockers help to keep things **organized**

**Clerestory** windows give both **light** and ventilation

**Dormitory** rooms provide **private** sleeping areas for visitors or care givers

**Access** to upper storage **spaces** can also be provided by a **stair**

The **volume** of a small house is **important** for a number of reasons:

1. Every cubic inch of the **interior** must be used as **efficiently** as possible including **multipurpose** living areas, storage, and work rooms

2. Natural **convection** and open ceilings keep rooms **cooler** in summer and capture **warm** air in the winter that can be **recirculated** with ceiling fans

3. Vertical **lines** of sight are created as upper and lower living areas **open** to each other, giving the **feeling** of a large room in a small house

4. Water lines and HVAC ducts are within the conditioned space to reduce heat and cooling loss

## A small house is built for living

A small house is multi-functional with a **modest** sense of **space** and a **well thought out** feeling for the **important** things that make a house a home.*

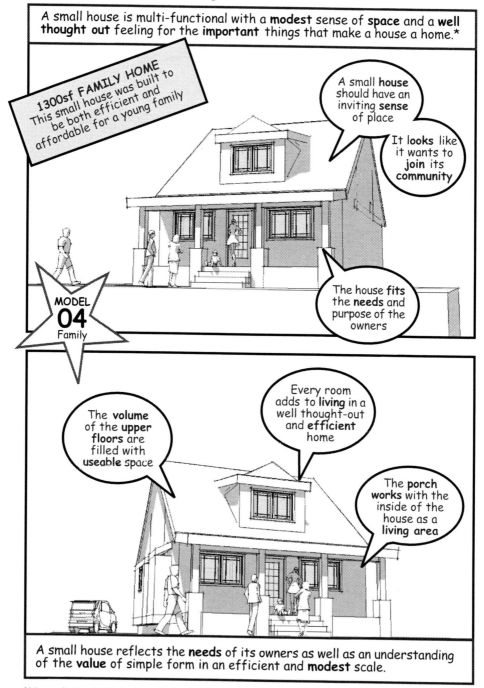

1300sf FAMILY HOME
This small house was built to be both efficient and affordable for a young family

MODEL
**04**
Family

A small **house** should have an inviting **sense** of place

It **looks** like it wants to **join** its **community**

The house **fits** the **needs** and purpose of the owners

The **volume** of the **upper floors** are filled with **useable** space

Every room adds to **living** in a well thought-out and **efficient** home

The **porch works** with the inside of the house as a **living area**

A small house reflects the **needs** of its owners as well as an understanding of the **value** of simple form in an efficient and **modest** scale.

*Home design by Rick Thompson, Architect.
See more at www.thompsonplans.com

**Multipurpose spaces fit the family's lifestyle**

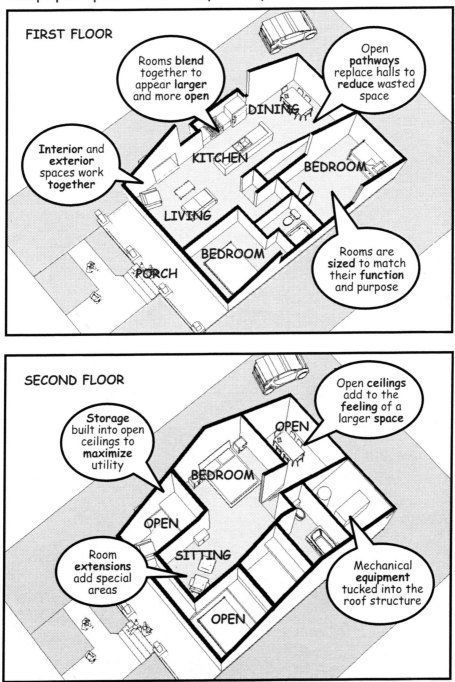

## A small house reflects purpose and function

In a **small house**, rooms must be **functional** and purposeful. Rooms are built to be **comfortable** and convenient with full use of **three-dimensional** space. The house **personifies** and embraces its family as a home.

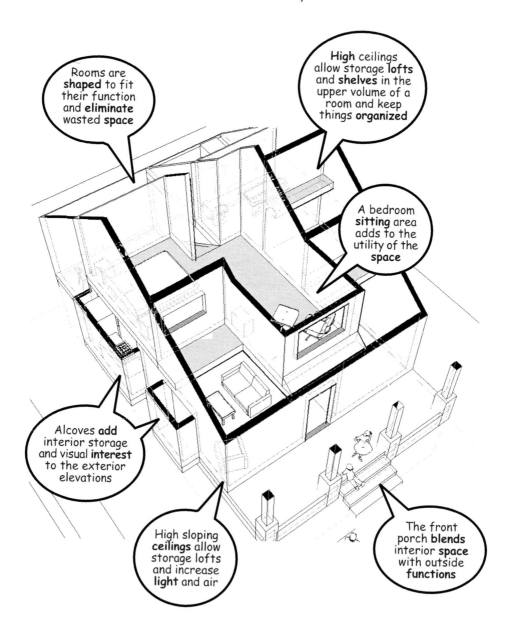

Rooms are **shaped** to fit their function and **eliminate** wasted **space**

**High** ceilings allow storage **lofts** and **shelves** in the upper volume of a room and keep things **organized**

A bedroom **sitting** area adds to the utility of the **space**

Alcoves **add** interior storage and visual **interest** to the exterior elevations

High sloping **ceilings** allow storage lofts and increase **light** and air

The front porch **blends** interior **space** with outside **functions**

# Features found in a small house

## Minimized for living

A small house must be purposeful with a well defined list of functions that it must fulfill

A small house reflects its purpose and the people who live in it

The owners must be self determined, no one is selling small and there are no sales features to chose

## Design

The rooms in the house must fit the activities and movement of the people who live in them

Flexibility is built into floors and walls so that the house can evolve and change with the family

Open multiple purpose rooms that can be used for different or simultaneous functions

Flexible furnishings that can be changed or rearranged as needs evolve

Vertical and horizontal sight lines with open and interesting use of three dimensional space

An open plan and high ceilings add a feeling of space to otherwise small activity areas

Clerestory windows and lofts make use of high sloping ceilings that can be used for day light and storage

Dormers and cantilevered alcoves add headroom and usable space to the interior

Designated storage areas with seasonal or long and short-term access

The volume of roofs and attics are used for living and storage

Outside spaces like porches are important extensions of indoor living and sleeping areas

Mechanical systems are easy to maintain and efficiently located within the house

The house must be built so it can be physically added to and modified as needs and purposes change

## Land use

The house can be built on a portion of a lot to leave plenty of room for the house to evolve and change

More than one small house can be built on a lot as a cluster of family units or affordable housing

Small houses require less maintenance and resources to maintain them

An ideal location for a small house is a plot of land in an existing neighborhood

The land and the house work together to support the purpose of the house

# CHAPTER THREE

## Surviving SMALL

The features found in small houses are rooted in the shelters used in historical settlements and homesteads. This can be seen in the shelter and security of the first settlements, then as small one room houses that protected settlers from their often brutal environment, and later as a sanctuary from which to simplify life's many challenges.

### Settlements

Early settlers migrating into a new territory had to be particularly adept at surviving as a community. For them the settlement was an outpost in an enclosed compound that could protect them from the dangers that surrounded them. Builders used tools and local resources to erect small houses as the settlement matured. These little houses provided a private place within the shared space of a larger gated community.

### Survival

Pioneers moved onto the frontiers and established homesteads deep in the wilderness of the USA. They built houses that helped them survive the rigors of life far away from civilization.

Later settlers like the Crackers in the south built homes closer to roads and towns where they had access to supplies, materials, and the skills necessary to make a comfortable start at a new life. Settlers used manufactured and local resources to build simple homes that could be modified and expanded as families and farms grew.

### Rediscovery

At the heart of all these small houses was a multipurpose single room that provided the basic necessities. These houses simplified life and helped people succeed in their broader effort at survival under difficult conditions.

Thoreau rediscovered this simple house-form when he built his retreat from civilization on the shores of Walden Pond. Here the construction of a single simple room with only the basic comforts provided him the focus he needed to rethink his place in a increasingly materialistic society.

## Early settlements were built from local resources

The first **settlements** in the USA were located on the banks of rivers that could provide transportation and protection. These were more **fortresses** than peaceful **communities**, with the river, adjacent swamps, and nearby forests used to sustain the **settlements**.*

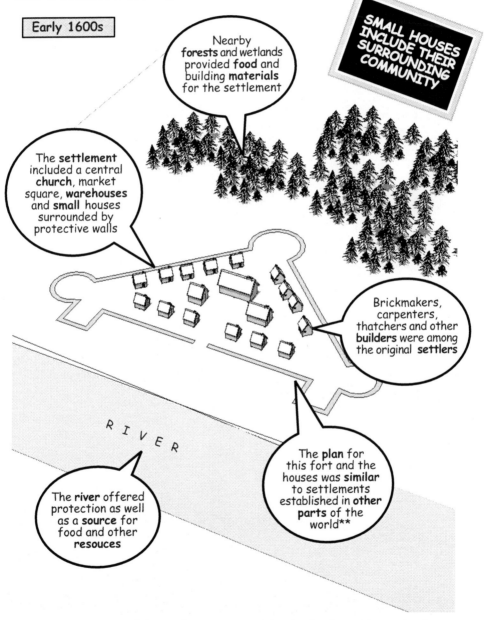

Early 1600s

Nearby **forests** and wetlands provided **food** and building **materials** for the settlement

SMALL HOUSES INCLUDE THEIR SURROUNDING COMMUNITY

The **settlement** included a central **church**, market square, **warehouses** and **small** houses surrounded by protective walls

Brickmakers, carpenters, thatchers and other **builders** were among the original **settlers**

RIVER

The **river** offered protection as well as a **source** for food and other **resouces**

The **plan** for this fort and the houses was **similar** to settlements established in **other parts** of the world**

The small house was part of gated community

This small house provided privacy within the community

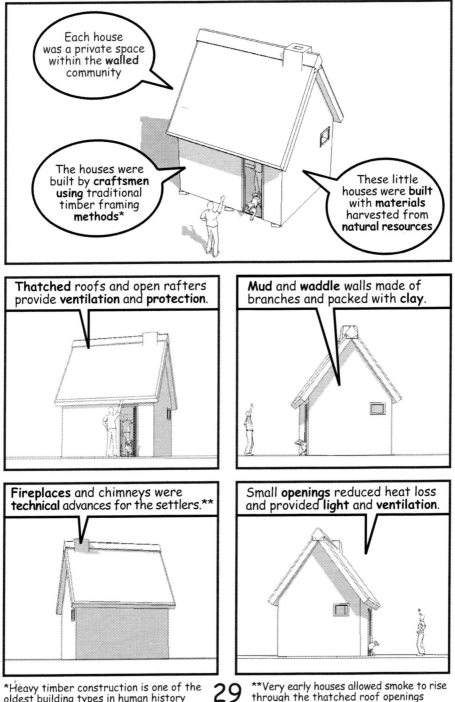

Each house was a private space within the **walled** community

The houses were built by **craftsmen using** traditional timber framing **methods***

These little houses were **built** with **materials** harvested from **natural resources**

**Thatched** roofs and open rafters provide **ventilation** and **protection**.

**Mud** and **waddle** walls made of branches and packed with **clay**.

**Fireplaces** and chimneys were **technical** advances for the settlers.**

Small **openings** reduced heat loss and provided **light** and **ventilation**.

*Heavy timber construction is one of the oldest building types in human history

29

**Very early houses allowed smoke to rise through the thatched roof openings

**Construction materials harvested from local resources**

Skilled **craftpersons** brought the **traditions** of **heavy timber** framing, brickmaking, iron working, and roof construction to **build** these little houses.*

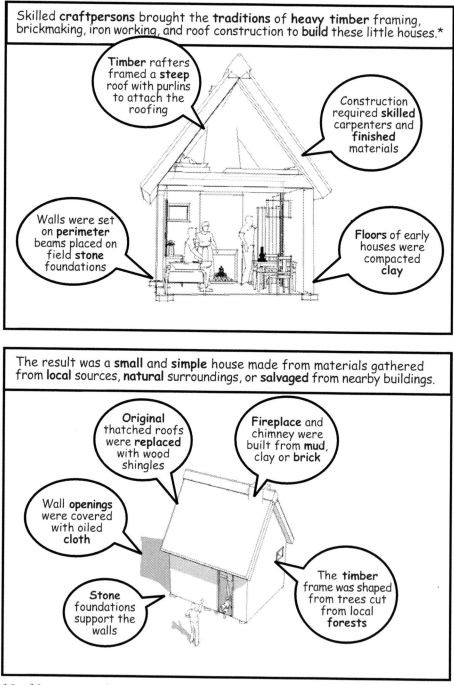

**Timber** rafters framed a **steep** roof with purlins to attach the roofing

Construction required **skilled** carpenters and **finished** materials

Walls were set on **perimeter** beams placed on field **stone** foundations

**Floors** of early houses were compacted **clay**

The result was a **small** and **simple** house made from materials gathered from **local** sources, **natural** surroundings, or **salvaged** from nearby buildings.

Original thatched roofs were **replaced** with wood shingles

**Fireplace** and chimney were built from **mud**, clay or **brick**

Wall **openings** were covered with oiled **cloth**

**Stone** foundations support the walls

The **timber** frame was shaped from trees cut from local **forests**

*See "Conservation of Historical Buildings"
Bernard Feilden for construction techniques 30

A small house meant living purposefully

These simple **little houses** provided **basic** shelter for settlers all along the frontier of the US from the early 1600s. They were **simple** spaces that included the bare **necessities** of life in a new world.*

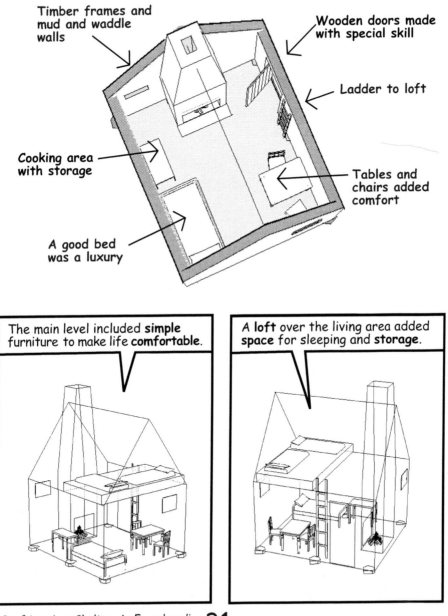

Timber frames and mud and waddle walls

Wooden doors made with special skill

Ladder to loft

Cooking area with storage

Tables and chairs added comfort

A good bed was a luxury

The main level included **simple** furniture to make life **comfortable**.

A **loft** over the living area added **space** for sleeping and **storage**.

*See "American Shelter: An Encyclopedia of American Homes" by Lester Walker

Skilled labor was required to build a small house

MODEL
**05**
Settlement

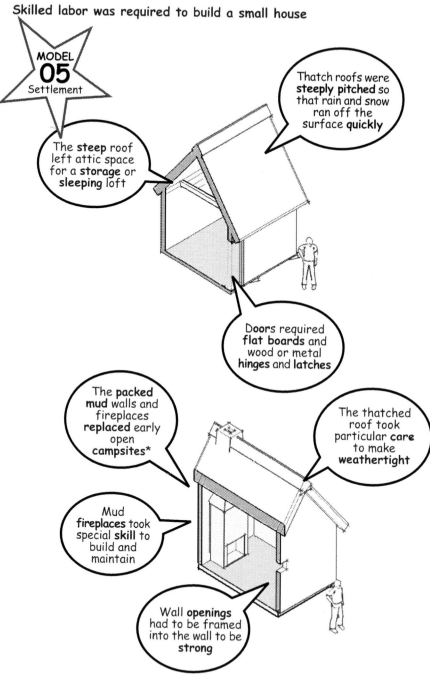

Thatch roofs were **steeply pitched** so that rain and snow ran off the surface **quickly**

The **steep** roof left attic space for a **storage** or **sleeping** loft

Doors required **flat boards** and wood or metal **hinges** and **latches**

The **packed mud** walls and fireplaces **replaced** early open campsites*

The thatched roof took particular **care** to make **weathertight**

Mud **fireplaces** took special **skill** to build and maintain

Wall **openings** had to be framed into the wall to be **strong**

# Houses were built from common materials and methods

The actual **sizes** of the settlement houses were not exactly the same. Each was **different**, depending on individual **need**. Construction **details** were **similar** however, **reflecting** the trades and traditions of the **craftsmen** who built them.

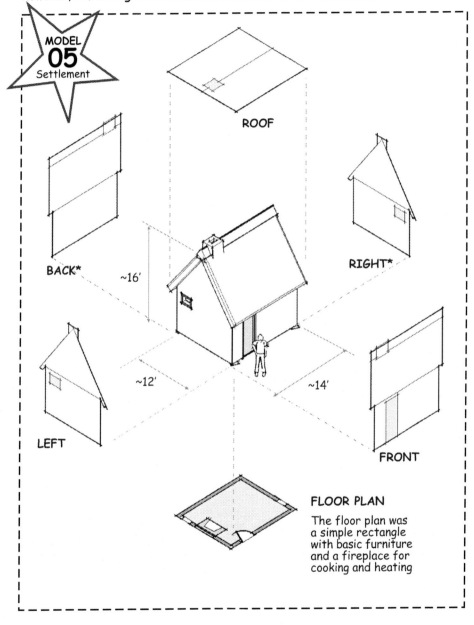

MODEL
**05**
Settlement

ROOF

BACK*

~16'

RIGHT*

LEFT

~12'

~14'

FRONT

FLOOR PLAN

The floor plan was a simple rectangle with basic furniture and a fireplace for cooking and heating

*These elevations are mirrored to make it easier to visualize the building elevations  33

## A settler's house on the frontier provided protection

The houses of the **pioneers** who moved onto the **frontiers** had to meet the basic needs of shelter and provide a place to **work** the land far **away** from support.

Early 1600s-Late 1700s

SMALL HOUSES BLEND INSIDE AND OUTSIDE SPACES

Living on the **edge** of civilization meant finding a **homesite** that could provide the **resources** necessary for survival

Local **woodlands** provided **fuel** for cooking and heating as well as **timber** for construction

**Streams** and springs provided **water** and attracted wildlife for food

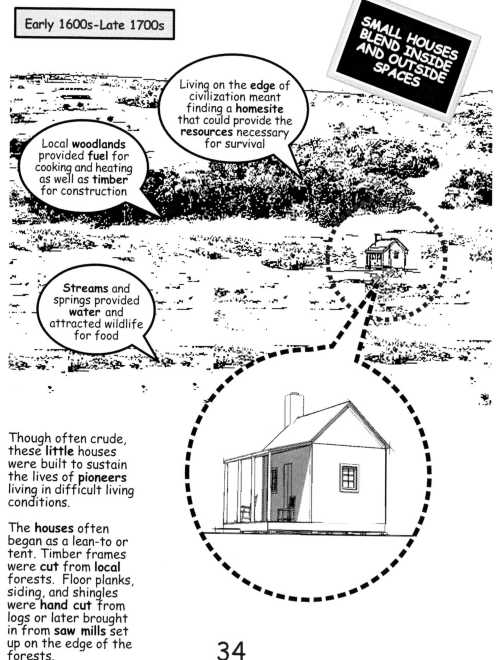

Though often crude, these **little** houses were built to sustain the lives of **pioneers** living in difficult living conditions.

The **houses** often began as a lean-to or tent. Timber frames were **cut** from **local** forests. Floor planks, siding, and shingles were **hand cut** from logs or later brought in from **saw mills** set up on the edge of the forests.

34

## The small house responded to its environment

Settlers lived in **crude** shelters and understood the land **before** they began construction. This helped them **build** a house that **responded** to its environment.

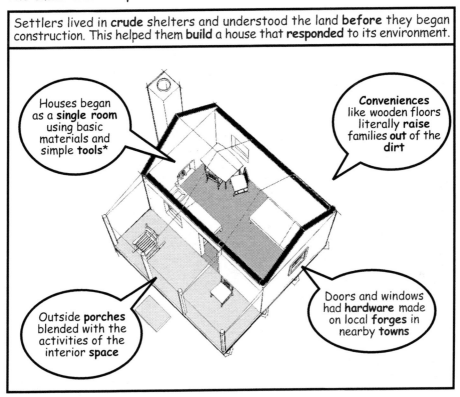

> Houses began as a **single room** using basic materials and simple **tools***

> **Conveniences** like wooden floors literally **raise** families **out** of the dirt

> Outside **porches** blended with the activities of the interior **space**

> Doors and windows had **hardware** made on local **forges** in nearby **towns**

South facing porches **shaded** walls from the sun and provided an outside **work area** that was a cooler place to **sit or sleep** in the summer.**

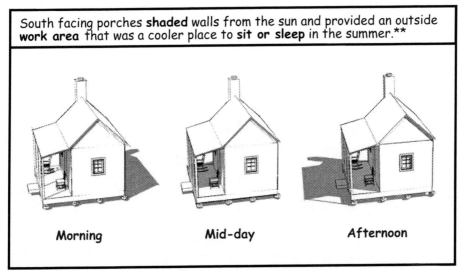

Morning          Mid-day          Afternoon

*The original single room house might also be converted to a cook house or utility shed

**Porches faced north in hotter climates in order to escape the summer sun

## A settler's house was built for shelter

Settlers that lived far away from established communities had to build **shelters** that both met basic needs and **supported** them while they worked.

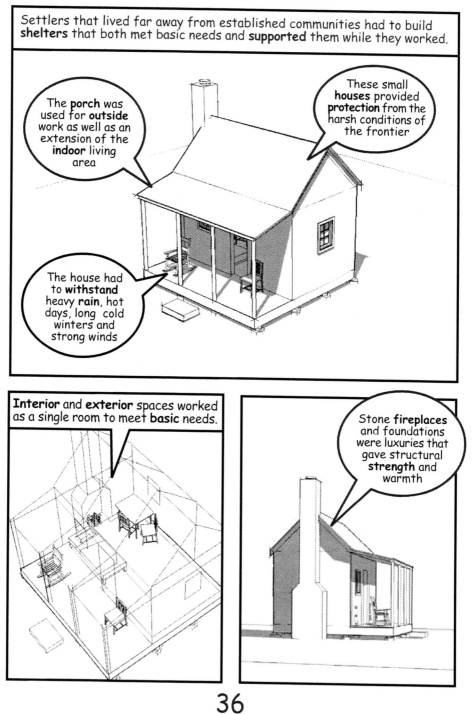

The **porch** was used for **outside** work as well as an extension of the **indoor** living area

These small **houses** provided **protection** from the harsh conditions of the frontier

The house had to **withstand** heavy **rain**, hot days, long cold winters and strong winds

**Interior** and **exterior** spaces worked as a single room to meet **basic** needs.

Stone **fireplaces** and foundations were luxuries that gave structural **strength** and warmth

Original shelters evolved with changing needs

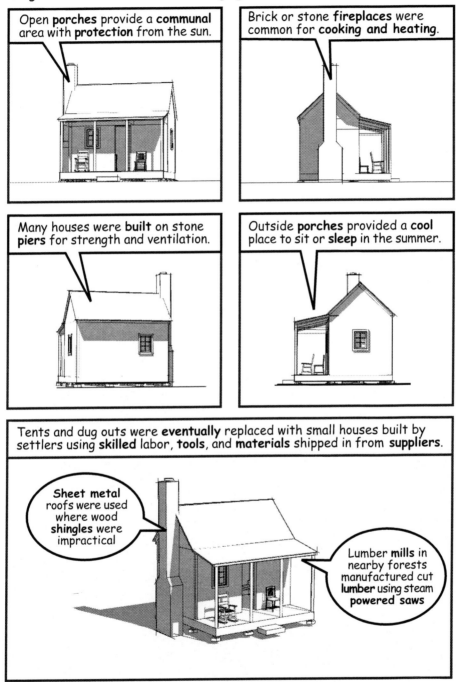

Open **porches** provide a **communal** area with **protection** from the sun.

Brick or stone **fireplaces** were common for **cooking and heating**.

Many houses were **built** on stone **piers** for strength and ventilation.

Outside **porches** provided a **cool** place to sit or **sleep** in the summer.

Tents and dug outs were **eventually** replaced with small houses built by settlers using **skilled** labor, **tools**, and **materials** shipped in from **suppliers**.

**Sheet metal** roofs were used where wood **shingles** were impractical

Lumber **mills** in nearby forests manufactured cut **lumber** using steam **powered saws**

37

### The settler's house introduced new construction techniques

These small houses provided **shelter** using a combination of **local** materials and **suppliers**. They were **innovative** in that they responded to their **environment** with **inventive** solutions using the basic **technologies** of their day.

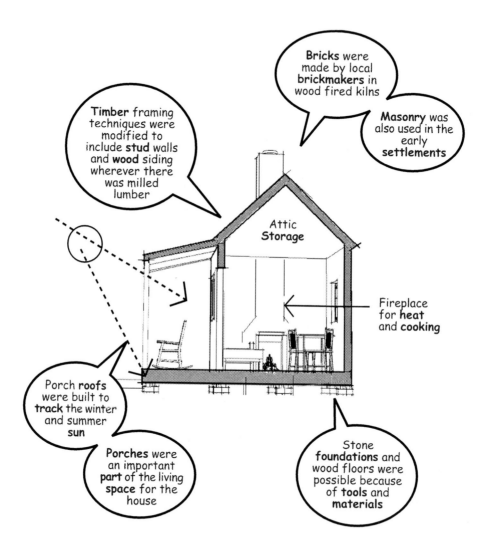

**Bricks** were made by local **brickmakers** in wood fired kilns

**Masonry** was also used in the early **settlements**

**Timber** framing techniques were modified to include **stud** walls and **wood** siding wherever there was milled lumber

Attic **Storage**

Fireplace for **heat** and **cooking**

Porch **roofs** were built to **track** the winter and summer **sun**

**Porches** were an important **part** of the living **space** for the house

Stone **foundations** and wood floors were possible because of **tools** and **materials**

These small houses reflect many different crafts

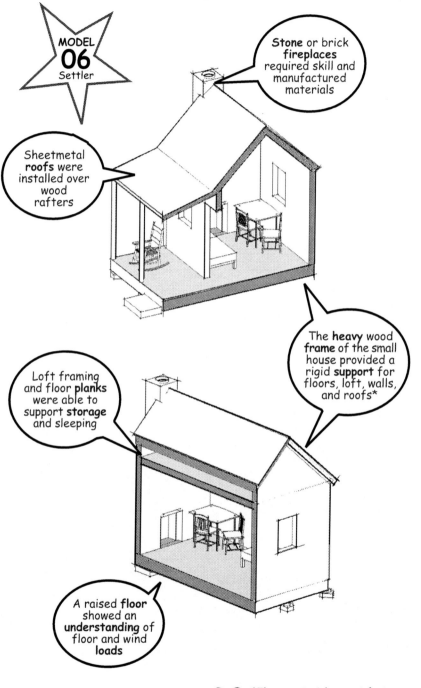

MODEL
**06**
Settler

Stone or brick **fireplaces** required skill and manufactured materials

Sheetmetal **roofs** were installed over wood rafters

The **heavy** wood **frame** of the small house provided a rigid **support** for floors, loft, walls, and roofs*

Loft framing and floor **planks** were able to support **storage** and sleeping

A raised **floor** showed an **understanding** of floor and wind **loads**

39  *These materials meant fastners and other hardware were available for construction

## Available resources shaped these small houses

Many of these **small** houses started as tent platforms. They **evolved** as porches were enclosed and rooms and **conveniences** were **added**. Construction mixed heavy timber **frames cut** from local forests with milled lumber from suppliers.

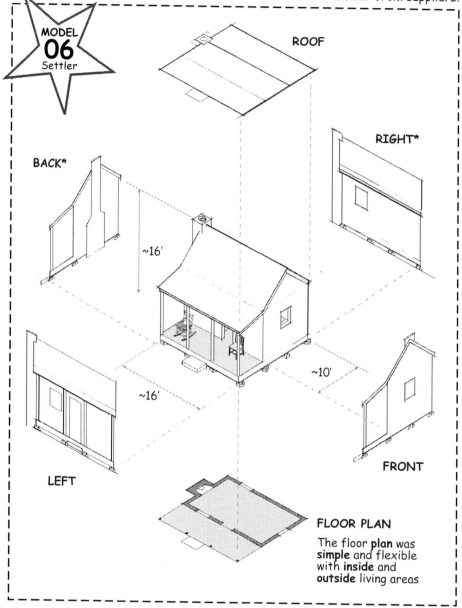

MODEL
**06**
Settler

ROOF

RIGHT*

BACK*

~16'

LEFT

~16'

~10'

FRONT

FLOOR PLAN

The floor **plan** was **simple** and flexible with **inside** and **outside** living areas

*These elevations are mirrored to make it easier to visualize the building elevations

### Cracker houses helped settle the deep south

Crackers were **settlers** who moved to the deep south of the USA. Their small houses were built to be a **working** part of a **homestead** and had a clear function as a one room shelter that **expanded** according to a family's needs*.

The 1800s

Homesteads were **subdivided** from large land **grants** to promote growth and **settlement**

CRACKERS BEGIN TO STANDARDIZE SMALL HOUSE CONSTRUCTION

The surrounding forest was an initial **source** of **food** and **materials**

The houses were set on **high** ground where a **clearing** could be cut

**Road** or trail access meant **products** could be shipped out and **materials** could be brought in

41  *See the book, "Classic Cracker: Florida's Wood Frame Vernacular" by Ronald Haase

**Porches were enclosed to add a new room**

**Porches** were an **important** part of a Cracker house. They **added** working **space** and could be **screened** or **enclosed** as the family and farm expanded.

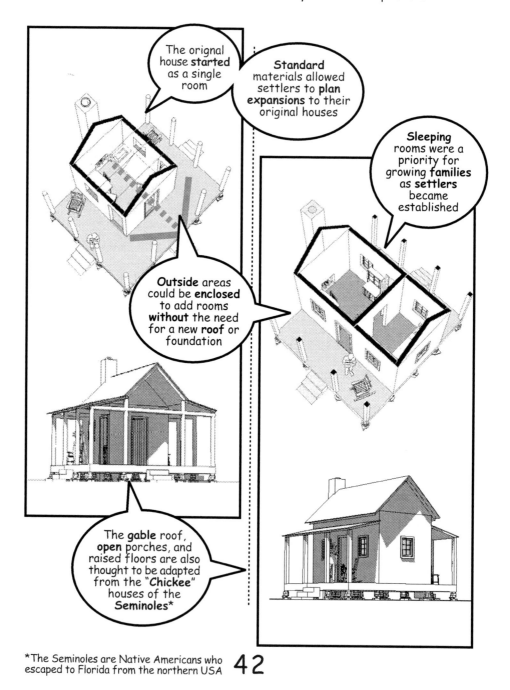

The orignal house **started** as a single room

**Standard** materials allowed settlers to **plan expansions** to their original houses

**Sleeping** rooms were a priority for growing **families** as **settlers** became established

**Outside** areas could be **enclosed** to add rooms **without** the need for a new **roof** or foundation

The **gable** roof, **open** porches, and raised floors are also thought to be adapted from the "**Chickee**" houses of the Seminoles*

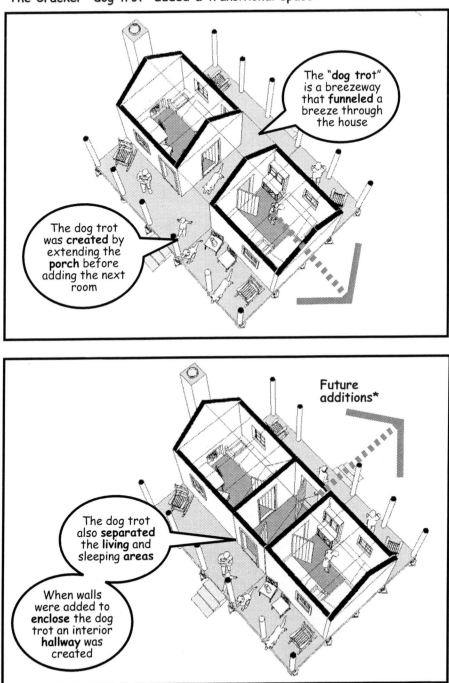

*Additions included bedrooms, cooking areas, or boarding rooms for passing travelers

Cracker houses were built to grow and expand*

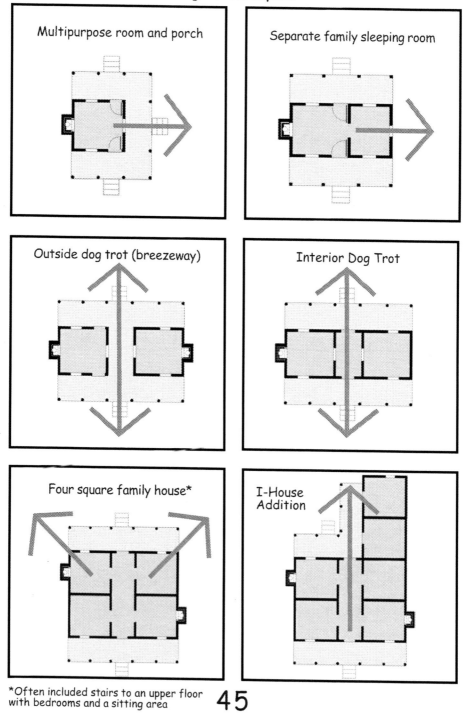

Multipurpose room and porch

Separate family sleeping room

Outside dog trot (breezeway)

Interior Dog Trot

Four square family house*

I-House Addition

*Often included stairs to an upper floor
with bedrooms and a sitting area

45

### Standard construction methods and materials

The details and **features** of the cracker vernacular indicate **common** construction materials and methods that were **sold** to settlers by independent **builders**.

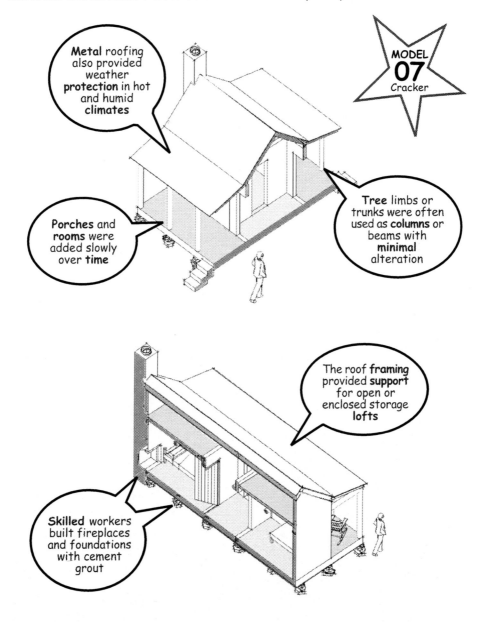

**Metal** roofing also provided weather **protection** in hot and humid **climates**

MODEL **07** Cracker

**Porches** and **rooms** were added slowly over **time**

**Tree** limbs or trunks were often used as **columns** or beams with **minimal** alteration

The roof **framing** provided **support** for open or enclosed storage **lofts**

**Skilled** workers built fireplaces and foundations with cement grout

Construction materials were available locally

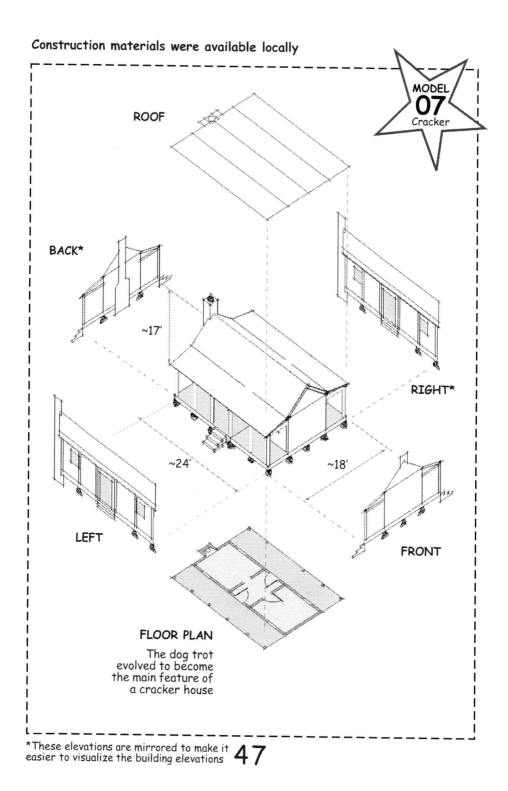

ROOF

BACK*

~17'

RIGHT*

LEFT

~24'

~18'

FRONT

FLOOR PLAN

The dog trot
evolved to become
the main feature of
a cracker house

MODEL
07
Cracker

## Living purposefully on Walden Pond

Henry David Thoreau **rediscovered** a **small** house when he built a **sanctuary** from his materialistic world and **found** the "necessities of a simple life."

Mid 1800s

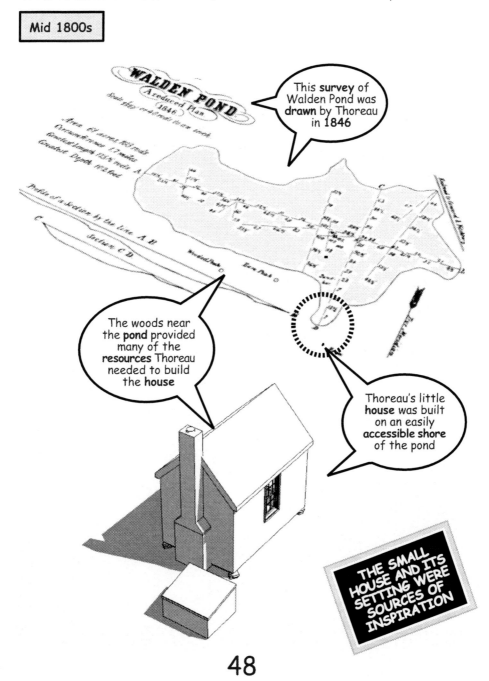

This **survey** of Walden Pond was **drawn** by Thoreau in **1846**

The woods near the **pond** provided many of the **resources** Thoreau needed to build the **house**

Thoreau's little **house** was built on an easily **accessible shore** of the pond

THE SMALL HOUSE AND ITS SETTING WERE SOURCES OF INSPIRATION

The site was not far from civilization

The house was **oriented** south with a view of the **pond**. Thoreau called the view a "**wall** of tranquility **surrounding** the house with its own sense of isolation."

*For detailed information see "Walden Pond: A History," by W. Barksdale Maynard

The **purpose** of Thoreau's house was to "**live** deliberately with only the bare **essentials** of **life** and see what **simplicity** had to teach."*

The **house** was 10' x 15' and was **built** from **local** materials

The house **sits** on a **simple** flat **stone** foundation

PURCHASED MATERIALS

Boards  $8.03
Roof/wall shingles  $4.00
Laths  $1.25
2 used windows  $2.43
1000 old brick  $4.00
2 casks of lime  $2.40
Hair  $0.31
Mantle-tree iron  $0.15
Nails  $3.90
Hinges and screws  $0.14
Latch  $0.10
Chalk  $0.01
Transportation  $1.40

Thoreau **gathered** stone, sand, and trees from the land for the house.

He **borrowed** an axe and **cut** tall pines in the nearby **woods** for **timber**.

He **added** a brick **chimney** and fireplace **after** the house was built.

The roof was **shingled** with the "first **slice**" of the **logs** used for the **frame**.

*Thoreau began the modern conservation movement with his book "Walden Pond"

## The small house mirrored Thoreau's simple life

Thoreau **built** the small house to distinguish "the **necessary** and the real" separating wants from **needs** in order "to see where your main **roots** run."

The house became a **sanctuary** as a space "...which **separates** a man from his fellows and makes him **solitary**"

To **"simplify** the problem of **life"** Thoreau included a table, chairs, bed and fireplace in a **minimal** space

Note there was **no porch** or intent to **expand** and settle

Boards were added to make the **attic** "useful for **storage**"

A **floor** hatch led to a **root** cellar for cold **storage**

He had **three** "chairs in the house; **one** for solitude, **two** for friendship, **three** for society."*

**51**

Thoreau was surprised at "how many great men and women a small house will contain."

**Features of a simple one room house**

Thoreau's **"necessary and real"** included a single room that provided the same **simple needs** important to the **lives** of early settlers and pioneers.

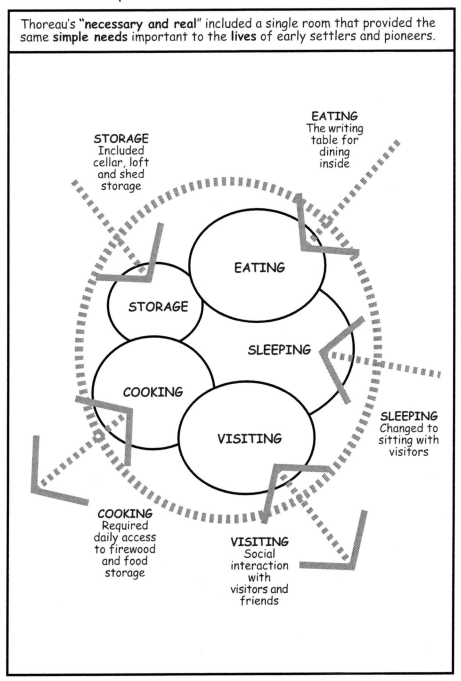

STORAGE
Included
cellar, loft
and shed
storage

EATING
The writing
table for
dining
inside

EATING

STORAGE

SLEEPING

COOKING

VISITING

SLEEPING
Changed to
sitting with
visitors

COOKING
Required
daily access
to firewood
and food
storage

VISITING
Social
interaction
with
visitors and
friends

**The small house was built to support simple needs**

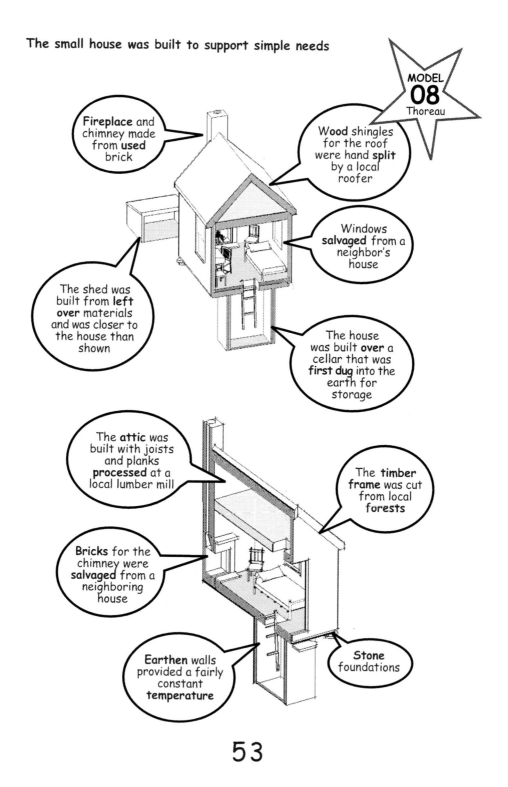

Fireplace and chimney made from **used** brick

Wood shingles for the roof were hand **split** by a local roofer

Windows **salvaged** from a neighbor's house

The shed was built from **left over** materials and was closer to the house than shown

The house was built **over** a cellar that was **first dug** into the earth for storage

The **attic** was built with joists and planks **processed** at a local lumber mill

The **timber frame** was cut from local **forests**

**Bricks** for the chimney were **salvaged** from a neighboring house

**Earthen** walls provided a fairly constant **temperature**

**Stone** foundations

53

These small houses were built for tough living

43 *The size of the house matched the needs of the immediate and extended family

## Building a sanctuary from a busy life

Thoreau built the house within walking distance of a **town** where he could find workers and materials. Lumber was **salvaged** from an abandoned house or cut and milled from **local** forests and built using **traditional** construction methods

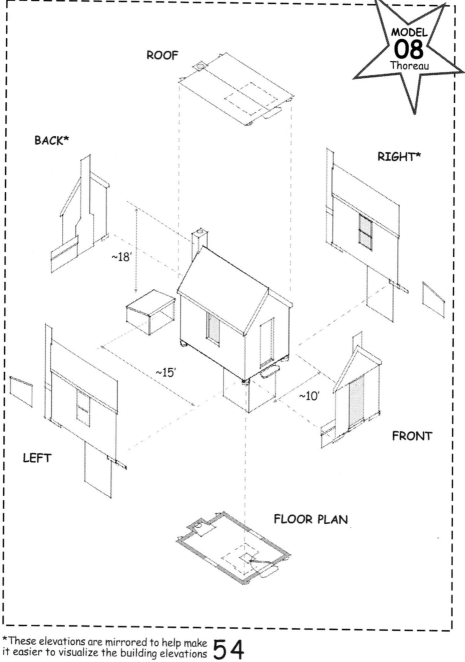

ROOF

MODEL
**08**
Thoreau

BACK*

RIGHT*

~18′

~15′

~10′

LEFT

FRONT

FLOOR PLAN

# CHAPTER FOUR
## Working SMALL

### Farmhouses
Settler houses grew to become small farm and ranch houses as demand for agricultural products increased and the family settled on the land.

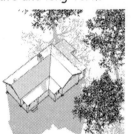

Farmhouses helped families work the land they had settled. They were built with a clear purpose and an understanding of their natural setting. This included a practical feel for the way the house was placed on the land. The house's relation to the work was also important to the immediate and long-term success of a farm.

### Worker housing
As farming operations expanded, small houses were built specifically for employees that worked on the farms or in one of the many related industries. Some of these were no more than shanties or abandoned buildings, but many were simple houses built in villages close to either the farm or town.

Worker housing provided a comfortable home for employees and their families along with close access to work. They were small and simple: two bedrooms, a kitchen, and a parlor with a porch.

### Company houses
Worker housing also included clusters of houses for families extracting resources in remote areas. These houses provided the same basic needs of other small houses, but were built more efficiently to lower cost and standardize amenities.

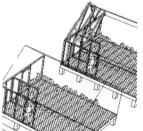

Almost identical floor plans and details lead to efficient production methods, a supply chain for construction materials, and prefabrication. This encouraged the growth of an industry that included suppliers, manufacturers, specialized trades, and skilled workers. An efficient construction industry meant homes could be produced economically and fast enough to meet a growing demand.

The farmhouse was the heart of the daily work

Mid-Late 1800s

DIRECT ACCESS TO WORK ADDED FUNCTION TO THE SMALL HOUSE

Difficult land was cleared last or used for grazing

Farmers lived in simple **shelters** until enough land could be **cleared** to support a family*

**Access** to work in the surrounding **fields** from the house was **important**

The farmhouse was at the **center** of the family's daily **activity**

The house was **clustered** with **sheds** and **barns** and farm animals

A nearby **road** provided **access** to **market** and supplies**

*See "The Farmhouse: Classic Homesteads of North America" by Nancy L. Mohr

**The best farmland often had the least natural resources for building a farmhouse

The house grew to meet the needs of the farm and family

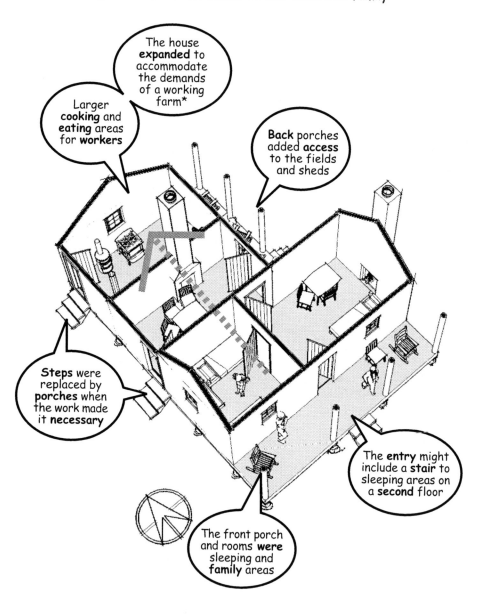

**The house was the center of the work**

Exterior **doors** provided direct **access** to each room in the house and **direct access** to barns, sheds, storage and equipment **outside** the house.

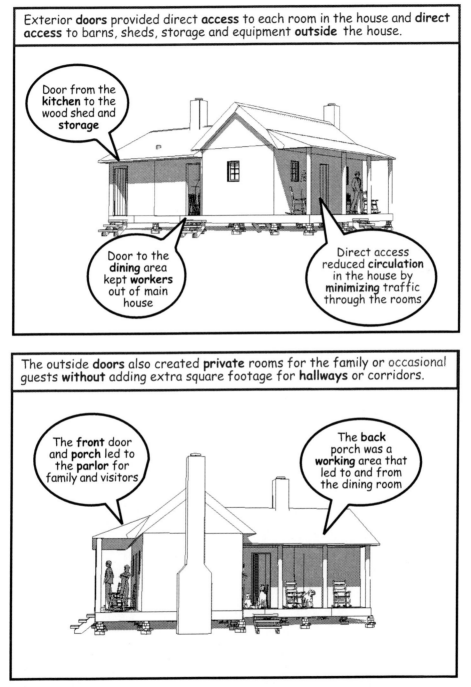

Door from the **kitchen** to the wood shed and **storage**

Door to the **dining** area kept **workers** out of main house

Direct access reduced **circulation** in the house by **minimizing** traffic through the rooms

The outside **doors** also created **private** rooms for the family or occasional guests **without** adding extra square footage for **hallways** or corridors.

The **front** door and **porch** led to the **parlor** for family and visitors

The **back** porch was a **working** area that led to and from the dining room

## The house reflected the pattern of work on the farm

Early farmhouses were located in **different** areas of the USA, but they **shared** many common **characteristics** because they were built for the same purpose:

1. They often evolved from small single room houses
2. The purpose of the house was to support the work
3. Outside spaces were as important as inside spaces
4. Rooms were added progressively as the farm and family grew

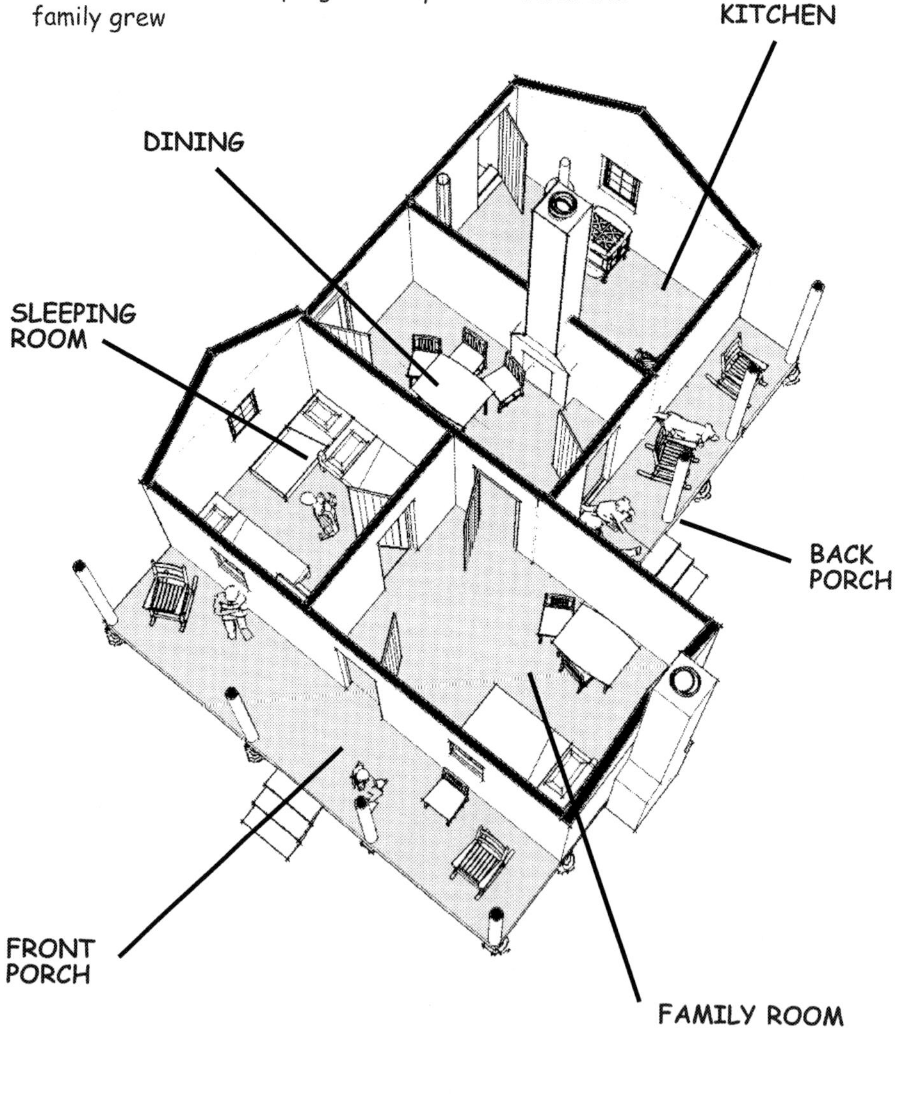

KITCHEN

DINING

SLEEPING ROOM

BACK PORCH

FRONT PORCH

FAMILY ROOM

Every addition required well planned construction

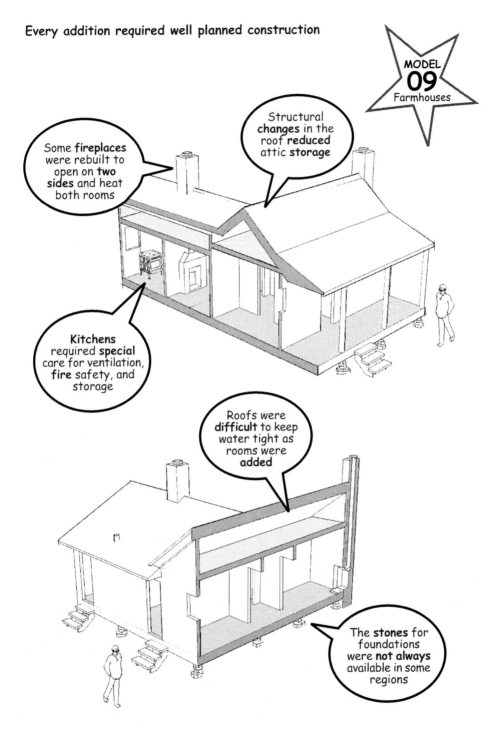

Structural **changes** in the roof **reduced** attic **storage**

Some **fireplaces** were rebuilt to open on **two sides** and heat both rooms

**Kitchens** required **special** care for ventilation, **fire** safety, and storage

Roofs were **difficult** to keep water tight as rooms were **added**

The **stones** for foundations were **not always** available in some regions

61

**Improvements to the house were built to meet new needs**

The changing **needs** of a growing farm shaped the house as the family **settled** on the land. Each change **filled** a new purpose directly **related** to the work.

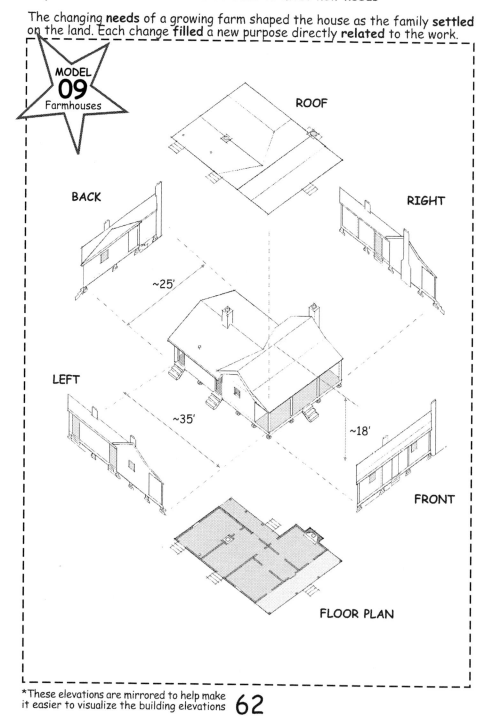

MODEL
**09**
Farmhouses

ROOF

BACK

RIGHT

~25'

LEFT

~35'

~18'

FRONT

FLOOR PLAN

*These elevations are mirrored to help make
it easier to visualize the building elevations

**A ranch house began with an understanding of the land**

Early ranchers used an **intuitive** understanding of the land to **locate** the **house** and outbuildings in the **best** possible **location** for the family and the work.

Mid to Late 1800s

SMALL HOUSES ADDED TO THE PROTECTION OF THE NATURAL ENVIRONMENT

Ranchers **working** the land started with a **campsite** that often became the future **homesite**

Existing **trees** and **terrain** offered natural **protection** from the wind and the sun

Natural **vegetation** could also be a **sign** of water and a good place to **dig** a well

**Water** and drainage were **important** to a successful **ranch**

**The ranch house literally grew from the land**

**Placement** of the original house was critical to the ranch's **success**. The house had to be close to the **work** but in an area where there was room for expansion.

ORIGINAL HOUSE

Fireplaces, porches, and foundations were **added** to the original house as the farm succeeded

Existing **vegetation** continued to **grow** as the house **expanded**

Planned **expansion** was important for the success of the farm

The **homesite** commonly **included** a kitchen **garden** as a source of food

Ranches produced **products** that could be taken to nearby **markets** on roads

ROAD

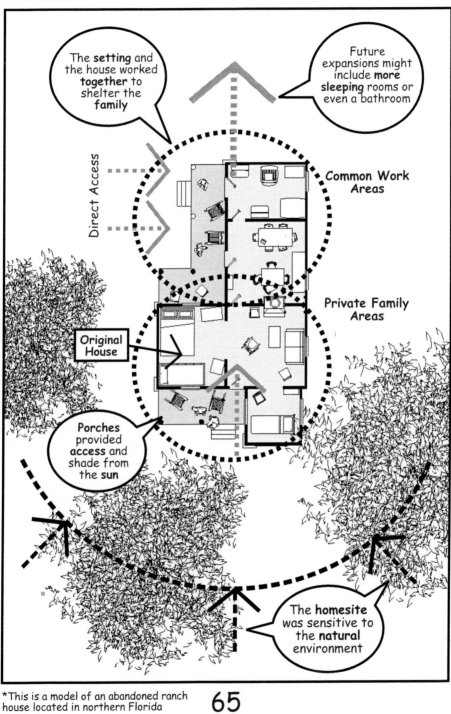

Shade trees grew along with the house

The house and homesite worked together

Building a ranch house required planning, intuition, and imagination

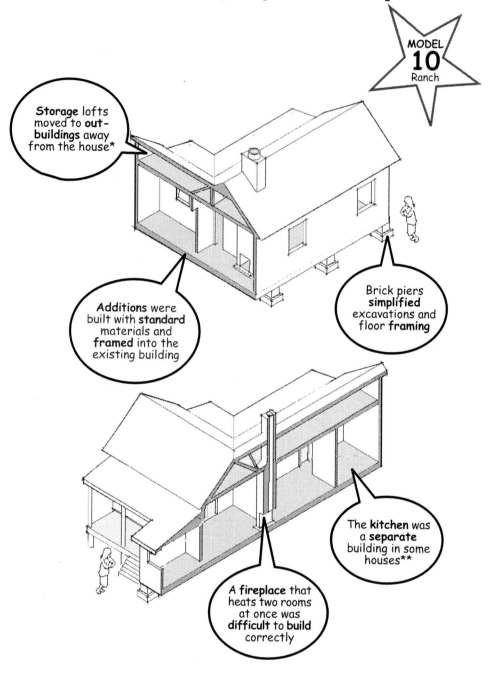

MODEL
**10**
Ranch

Storage lofts moved to **out-buildings** away from the house*

Additions were built with **standard** materials and **framed** into the existing building

Brick piers **simplified** excavations and floor **framing**

The **kitchen** was a **separate** building in some houses**

A **fireplace** that heats two rooms at once was **difficult** to **build** correctly

## Built by practical owners for practical purposes

A **ranch house** was built to **provide** shelter and a place to **sleep** and **eat** out of the weather. **Every board** in the house was **nailed** in place with this **purpose**.

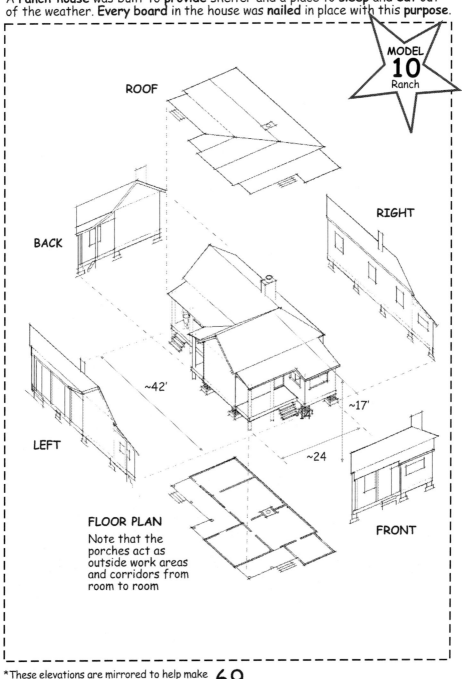

MODEL
**10**
Ranch

ROOF

BACK

RIGHT

LEFT

~42'

~17'

~24

FLOOR PLAN

Note that the porches act as outside work areas and corridors from room to room

FRONT

**Local farms and ranches provided food for city centers**

As farms and towns **expanded**, houses were built for workers on unproductive land or along **roads** that were used to bring **food** and other **goods** to market.*

Mid-Late 1800s

Houses for workers were often built **near town** or in a **cluster** of houses surrounded by the fields

**Access** to the **city** was important in order to **transport** products and **buy** supplies

SMALL HOUSES FILLED THE NEED FOR WORKER HOUSING

The **barn** and stables were often more **important** than the house

Fields were **worked** with horse drawn **plows** and wagons

**Small** houses were built to provide practical and **comfortable** shelter.

**Materials** included **manufactured** finishes, cabinets, and windows.

*See "The Farmhouse, Classic Homesteads of North America" by Nancy Mohr

70

The small house included modern conveniences

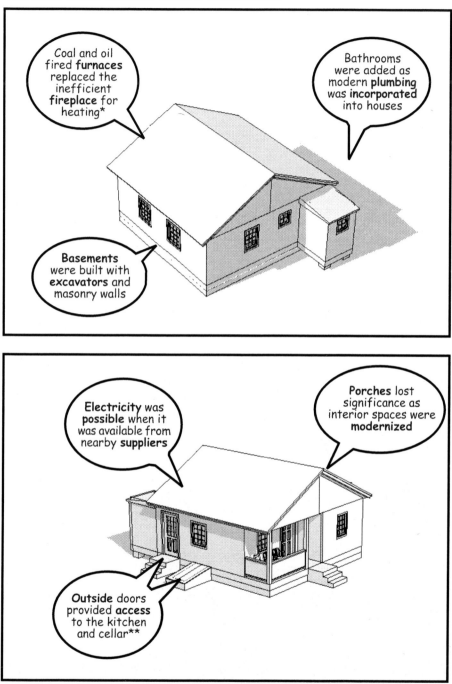

## Separate rooms for separate activities

**Rooms** began to be organized into **separate** bedrooms and closets with **modern** kitchens that were **open** to the dining and living areas to **maximize** floor space.

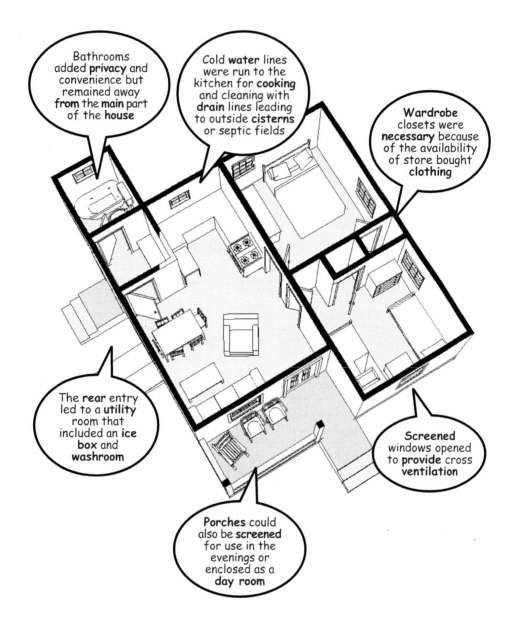

Bathrooms added **privacy** and convenience but remained away **from** the **main** part of the **house**

Cold **water** lines were run to the kitchen for **cooking** and cleaning with **drain** lines leading to outside **cisterns** or septic fields

**Wardrobe** closets were **necessary** because of the availability of store bought **clothing**

The **rear** entry led to a **utility** room that included an **ice box** and **washroom**

Screened windows opened to **provide** cross **ventilation**

**Porches** could also be **screened** for use in the evenings or enclosed as a **day room**

With **steady** employment, workers and their families were able to buy more products. This made **storage** space a **necessity** even in a small house.

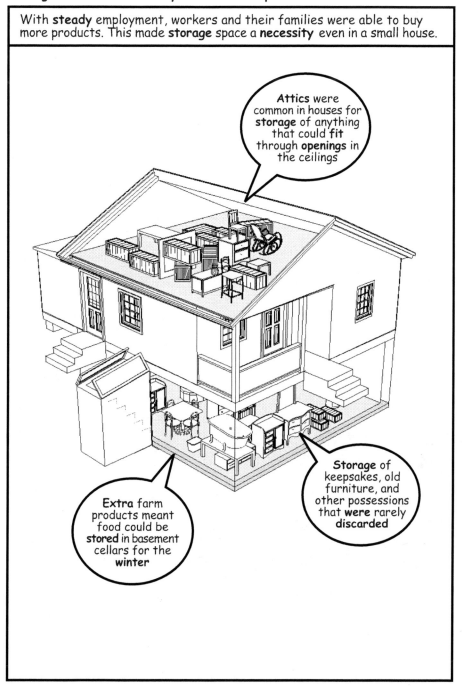

**Attics** were common in houses for **storage** of anything that could **fit** through **openings** in the ceilings

**Storage** of keepsakes, old furniture, and other possessions that **were** rarely **discarded**

**Extra** farm products meant food could be **stored** in basement cellars for the **winter**

73

# Technical innovation improved living conditions

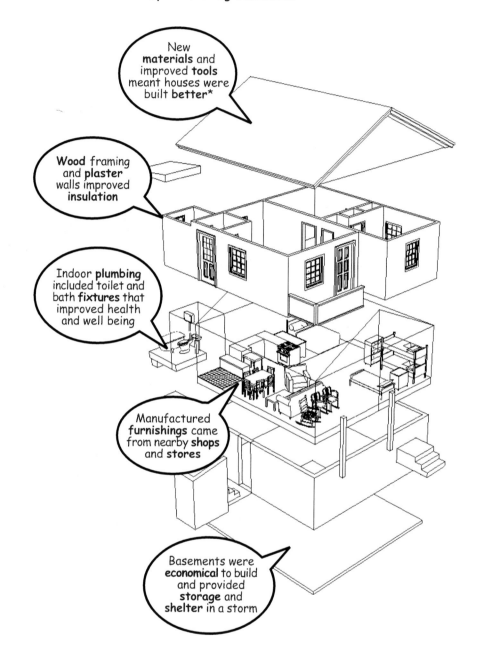

Home building becomes a service industry

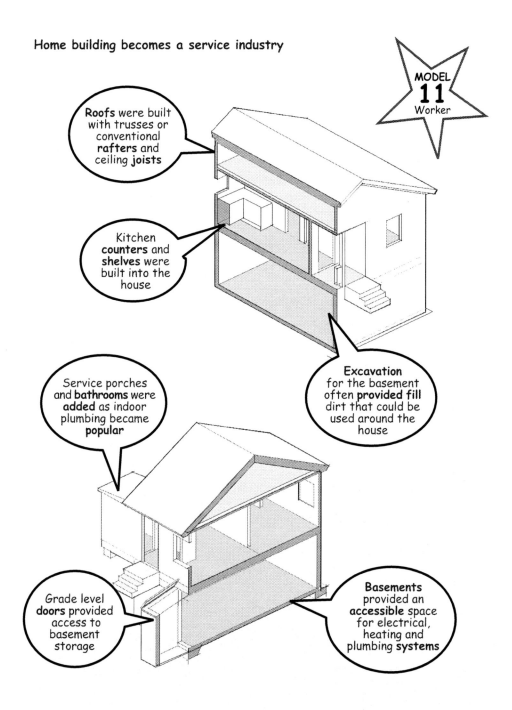

Roofs were built with trusses or conventional **rafters** and ceiling **joists**

Kitchen **counters** and **shelves** were built into the house

**Excavation** for the basement often **provided fill** dirt that could be used around the house

Service porches and **bathrooms** were **added** as indoor plumbing became **popular**

Grade level **doors** provided access to basement storage

**Basements** provided an **accessible** space for electrical, heating and plumbing **systems**

MODEL
**11**
Worker

## Small houses were built as a complete package

Houses built specifically for **workers** indicated the growing need to provide families with a plot of **land** and a **comfortable** home with modern **conveniences**.

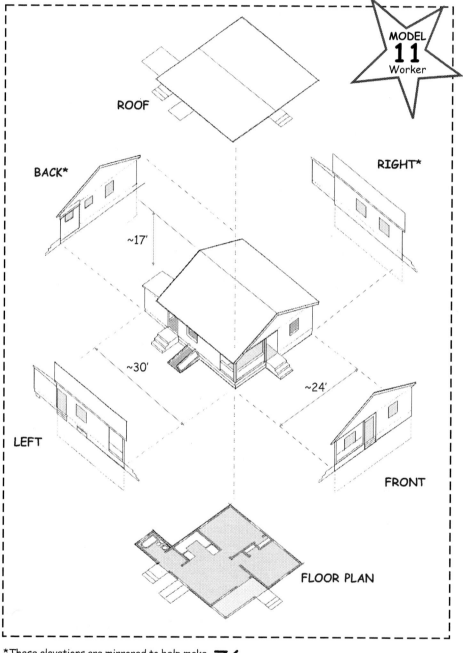

ROOF

MODEL
**11**
Worker

BACK*

RIGHT*

~17'

~30'

~24'

LEFT

FRONT

FLOOR PLAN

*These elevations are mirrored to help make it easier to visualize the building elevations

## Worker housing was the backbone of industrialization

**Housing** was built along **roadsides** for **tenants** and other **workers** on large farms, ranches, plantations, logging, and **camps** to improve access to production.

Late 1800-Early 1900s

**Worker** housing could also be **scattered** across the land and **poorly** maintained*

SMALL HOUSES HELPED SHAPE STANDARD METHODS AND MATERIALS

The **location** for worker housing depended on **available land** and access to the **work**

**Access** to the work **improved** production efficiency

*This was especially true of slave quarters on plantations throughout the southern USA

**Efficient housing was part of an efficient company**

Providing **housing** for workers in remote areas made good **business** sense. The small houses provided **shelter** and encouraged long-term employment.

Construction materials and methods were **standardized** to reduce cost

**Repetitive** details increased **efficiency** through repetitive tasks

The house also standardized **social** relationships because of **similar** layouts

The **house** was built to **maximize** the use of space and provide the **minimum** square footage necessary for **privacy**, comfort, and employee **satisfaction**.

Small houses could be **lifted** and **moved** to support operations in other **locations**

**Builders** could use precut pieces and specialized **labor** to **produce** housing at competitive prices

## Decent housing was important to employee production

Though **worker housing** was **better** than the early settler **houses**, only the **best** companies **provided** quality housing. **Most** labor camps included only the **bare necessities** with little regard for community or the surrounding environment.

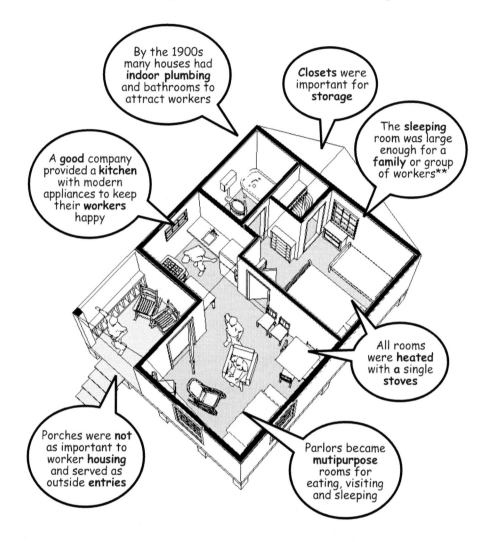

By the 1900s many houses had **indoor plumbing** and bathrooms to attract workers

**Closets** were important for **storage**

The **sleeping** room was large enough for a **family** or group of workers**

A **good** company provided a **kitchen** with modern appliances to keep their **workers** happy

All rooms were **heated** with **a single stoves**

Porches were **not** as important to worker **housing** and served as outside **entries**

Parlors became **mutipurpose** rooms for eating, visiting and sleeping

Construction took full **advantage** of prefabricated and manufactured materials like windows, plumbing, and cabinets to cut time and improve **efficiency**.

*See "Housing the Workers, 1850-1914: A Comparative Perspective," M.J. Daunton

**79**

**Dormitories or bunk houses were usually available for workers without families

## Manufactured construction materials were widely available

Innovations in materials and the organization of trades and labor helped create the standard methods now used by the construction industry.

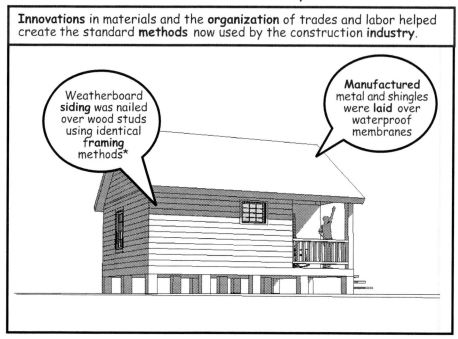

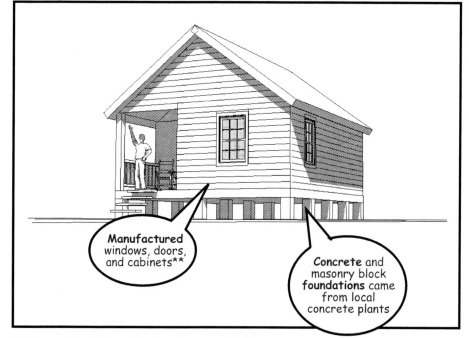

*Made possible with stock lumber sizes cut with new power tools at lumber mills

**These items were purchased from local suppliers, traveling salesmen, or mail order

## Housing production included many different trades

Housing could now be **produced** according to **predictable** practices that used **standard** materials and sizes. Labor was organized according to **specialized** trades and a **work breakdown structure** that divided the work into phases.

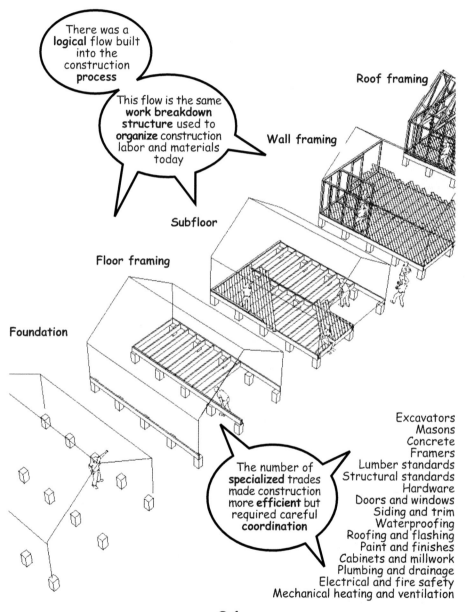

There was a **logical** flow built into the construction **process**

This flow is the same **work breakdown structure** used to **organize** construction labor and materials today

Roof framing

Wall framing

Subfloor

Floor framing

Foundation

The number of **specialized** trades made construction more **efficient** but required careful **coordination**

Excavators
Masons
Concrete
Framers
Lumber standards
Structural standards
Hardware
Doors and windows
Siding and trim
Waterproofing
Roofing and flashing
Paint and finishes
Cabinets and millwork
Plumbing and drainage
Electrical and fire safety
Mechanical heating and ventilation

Organized methods reduced cost and increased efficiency

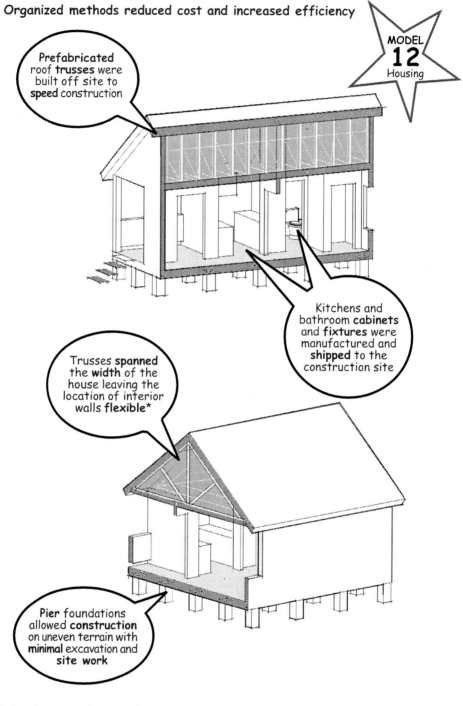

Prefabricated roof **trusses** were built off site to **speed** construction

MODEL
**12**
Housing

Kitchens and bathroom **cabinets** and **fixtures** were manufactured and **shipped** to the construction site

Trusses **spanned** the **width** of the house leaving the location of interior walls **flexible***

Pier foundations allowed **construction** on uneven terrain with **minimal** excavation and **site work**

*This also meant the shell of the house could be enclosed quickly in bad weather

## Worker housing helped perfect mass production methods

House construction in company camps and towns **helped** perfect the **systems** that evolved into the **mass production** methods used by the industry today.

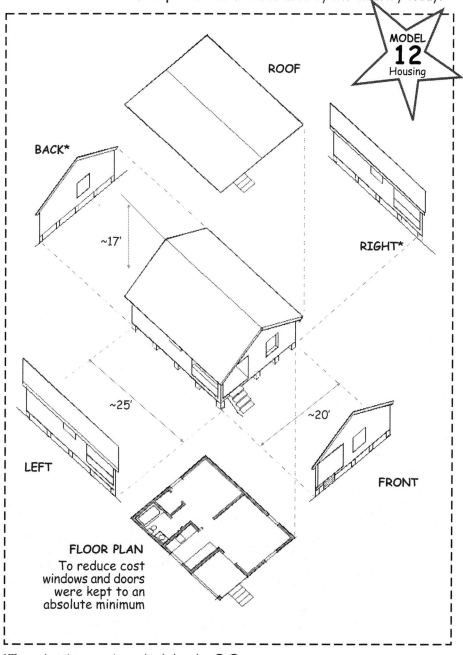

ROOF

MODEL
**12**
Housing

BACK*

~17'

RIGHT*

LEFT

~25'

~20'

FRONT

FLOOR PLAN
To reduce cost
windows and doors
were kept to an
absolute minimum

# CHAPTER FIVE

## Developing SMALL

The demand for worker housing was also increasing in towns near shipping ports and railroad depots. At first, houses were built to meet demand with isolated clusters of houses, but growth and industrialization made it necessary to develop entire neighborhoods.

The density of these developments contrasted sharply with the houses of early settlers and farmers, but the layout of plans for these houses reflected many of the same basic needs.

### Townhouses
Where very high density was required, small multi-story townhouses called "band boxes" were packed tightly onto congested streets creating very crowded neighborhoods.*

### Shotguns
In other cities, shotguns were built on narrow lots on the outskirts of the city to maximize density and affordability for needed workers. Many of these houses were built as one or two room starter homes and were slowly expanded over time. Blocks of shotgun houses were squeezed together so closely that occupants could reach out windows and touch their neighbors.

### Market Products
The density generated by these houses created oppressive living conditions. For those that could afford it, escape from city living came in the form of new communities built farther from the city center. These were planned communities with stylized houses built on plots of land that could be decorated and landscaped to meet the tastes of the owners.

With the popularity of the automobile, the demand for housing quickly evolved into a market for mass produced houses. Developers responded by supplying large tracts of housing at competitive prices.

* Bandboxes were hat boxes that were tied together in a stack for easy carrying

# Townhouses provided housing close to work

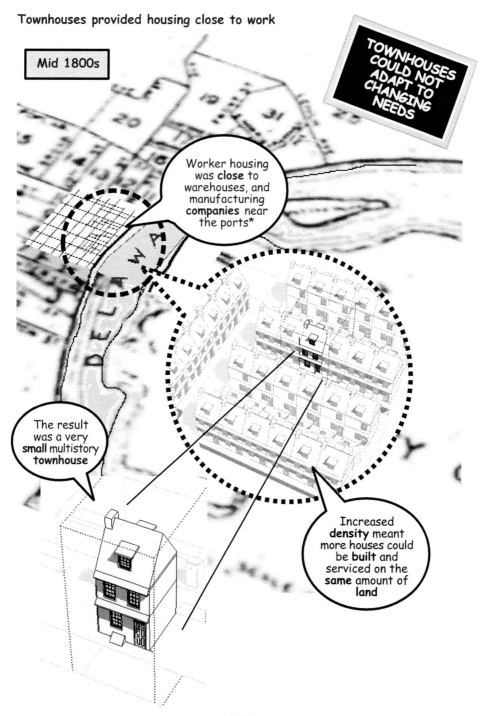

Mid 1800s

TOWNHOUSES COULD NOT ADAPT TO CHANGING NEEDS

Worker housing was **close** to warehouses, and manufacturing **companies** near the ports*

The result was a very **small** multistory **townhouse**

Increased **density** meant more houses could be **built** and serviced on the **same** amount of **land**

Townhouses maximized land use

## High density created many social challenges

Most townhouses were built simultaneously by the **same developer**, but a few were built **individually** on residential tracts **subdivided** by early city planners.

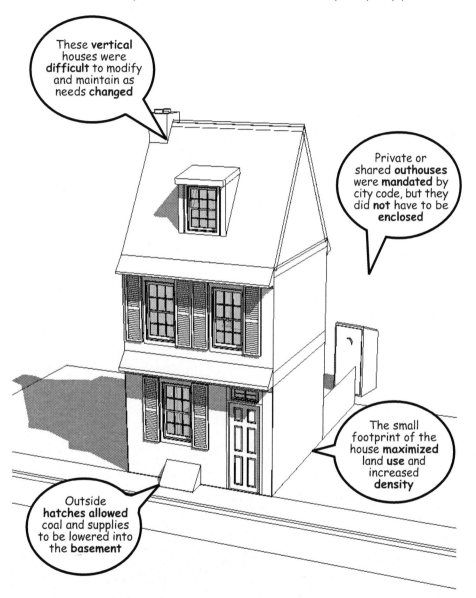

These **vertical** houses were **difficult** to modify and maintain as needs **changed**

Private or shared **outhouses** were **mandated** by city code, but they did **not** have to be **enclosed**

The small footprint of the house **maximized** land **use** and increased **density**

Outside **hatches allowed** coal and supplies to be lowered into the **basement**

**Living in a vertical house was a challenge**

Often referred to as **bandboxes**, these houses were built to be affordable. The street level room was used as a **shop** and attics were **rented** to **tenants**.

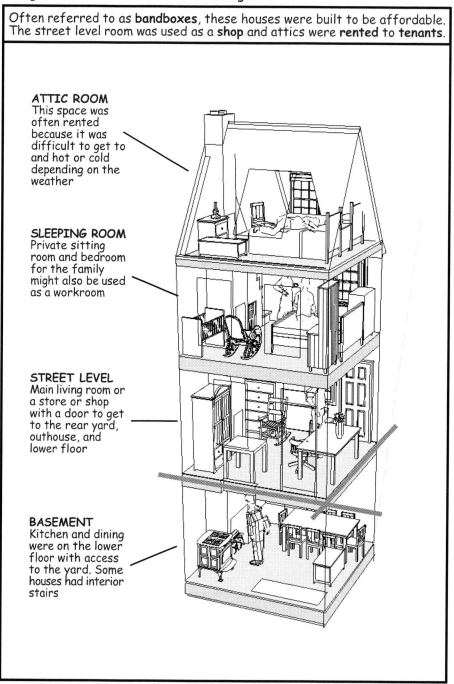

**ATTIC ROOM**
This space was often rented because it was difficult to get to and hot or cold depending on the weather

**SLEEPING ROOM**
Private sitting room and bedroom for the family might also be used as a workroom

**STREET LEVEL**
Main living room or a store or shop with a door to get to the rear yard, outhouse, and lower floor

**BASEMENT**
Kitchen and dining were on the lower floor with access to the yard. Some houses had interior stairs

**Building a vertical house was a challenge**

The key to the townhouse was the **stairs** that **provide access** from floor to floor. These **stairs** had to be carefully built into **limited** floor space.

Tall **chimneys** took special care to **construct** and **maintain***

Steep stairs evolved from loft **ladders** found in early settlement houses

The **stairs** to the attic room could be very **steep** and **difficult** to use

The **space** under the stairs could be used for **storage**

**Outside** stairs to the **kitchen increased** floor space on the **main** floor

# Townhouses required skilled construction workers

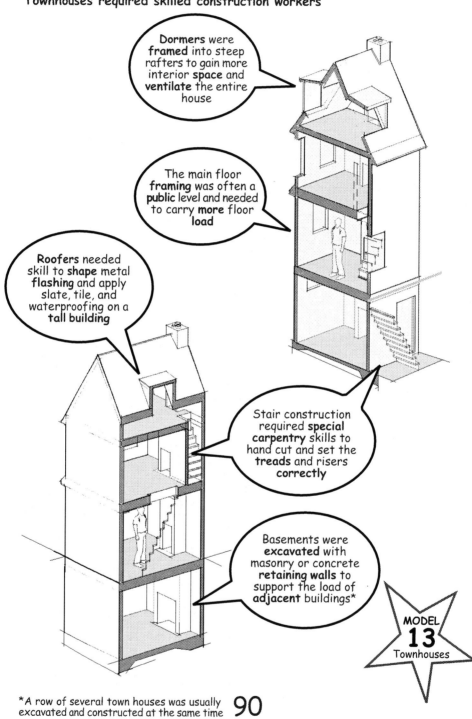

**Dormers** were **framed** into steep rafters to gain more interior **space** and **ventilate** the entire house

The main floor **framing** was often a **public** level and needed to carry **more** floor **load**

**Roofers** needed skill to **shape** metal **flashing** and apply slate, tile, and waterproofing on a **tall building**

Stair construction required **special carpentry** skills to hand cut and set the **treads** and risers **correctly**

Basements were **excavated** with masonry or concrete **retaining walls** to support the load of **adjacent** buildings*

MODEL
**13**
Townhouses

*A row of several town houses was usually excavated and constructed at the same time

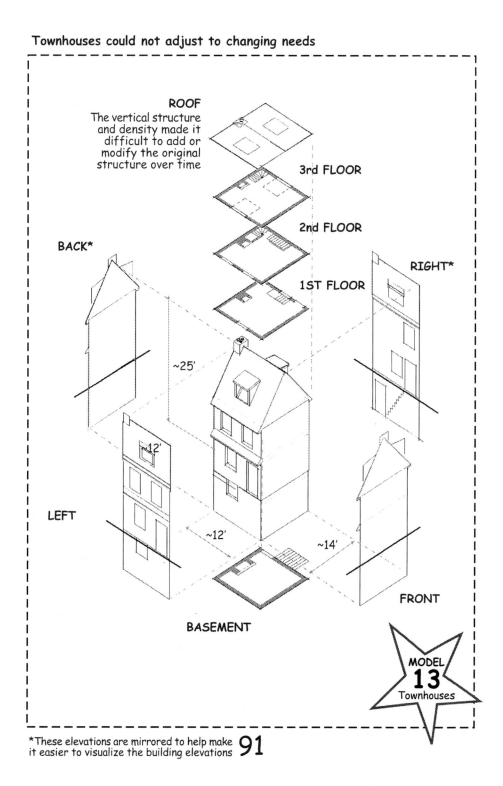

ROOF
The vertical structure and density made it difficult to add or modify the original structure over time

3rd FLOOR

2nd FLOOR

1ST FLOOR

BACK*

RIGHT*

~25'

~12'

LEFT

~12'

~14'

FRONT

BASEMENT

MODEL
13
Townhouses

*These elevations are mirrored to help make it easier to visualize the building elevations

91

**Worker housing needed to be flexible**

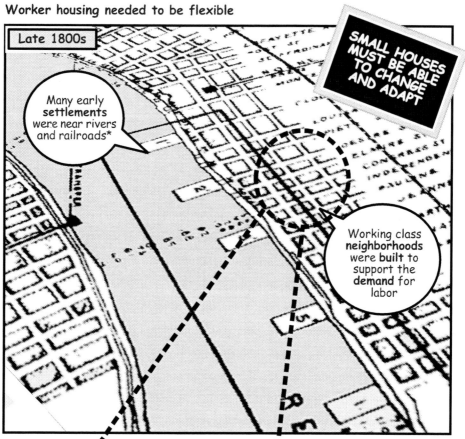

Working class **neighbor-hoods** were built on the outskirts of **towns** to house workers.

These houses were built to provide basic **services** and easy **access** to work at the lowest possible cost.

High **density** planning and **efficient** construction made the houses economical to service as well as **affordable** for working families to **buy**.

Over time, these houses were changed to meet the purpose and needs of their **owners**.

*Map adapted from 1892 survey by the Corp of Engineers, New Orleans District

## Shotguns were built to be affordable

These **small** houses were called **shotguns** because they were **long** and **narrow**. They were built to provide **low cost** housing for workers in the city.*

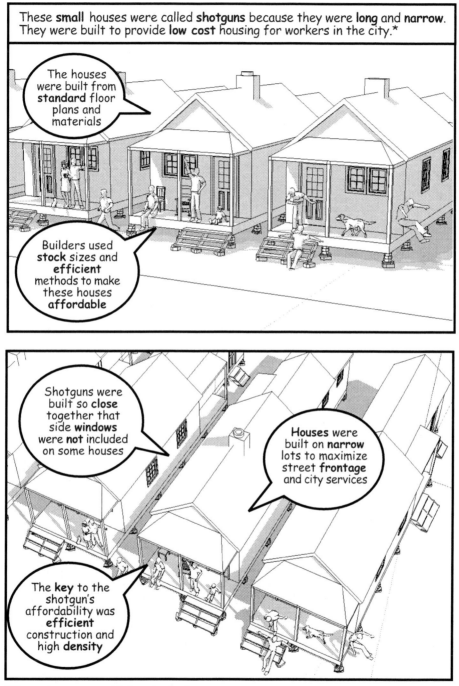

## Modifications to the small house made it sustainable

Shotguns took the **same rooms** found in other small houses and **adapted** them to long and narrow city lots. Interior spaces were **lined up** with doors connecting one room to another. **Pathways** within the rooms acted as corridors for circulation.

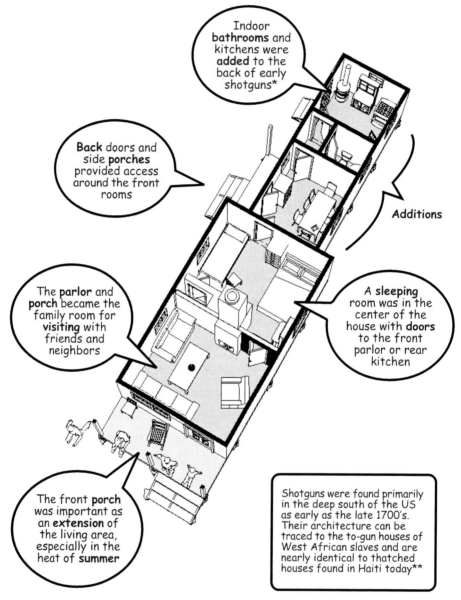

Indoor **bathrooms** and kitchens were **added** to the back of early shotguns*

**Back** doors and side **porches** provided access around the front rooms

Additions

The **parlor** and **porch** became the family room for **visiting** with friends and neighbors

A **sleeping** room was in the center of the house with **doors** to the front parlor or rear kitchen

The front **porch** was important as an **extension** of the living area, especially in the heat of **summer**

Shotguns were found primarily in the deep south of the US as early as the late 1700's. Their architecture can be traced to the to-gun houses of West African slaves and are nearly identical to thatched houses found in Haiti today**

*Early shotguns shared common outhouses and drinking wells with outdoor cooking areas

94

**See "Sources of the Shotgun House." by J.M. Vlach, Indiana University, March, 1975

Sidehall shotguns increased privacy

**Some shotguns added a second floor to meet changing needs**

**Built with methods and materials that could be changed**

It was easy to **add** rooms and **modify** the shotgun because the house was **built** on a raised pier foundation using **standard** materials and wood framing methods.

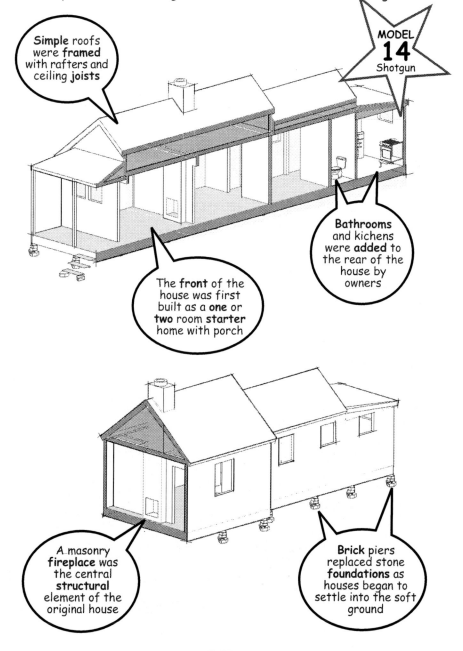

Simple roofs were **framed** with rafters and ceiling **joists**

MODEL **14** Shotgun

The **front** of the house was first built as a **one** or **two** room **starter** home with porch

**Bathrooms** and kichens were **added** to the rear of the house by owners

A masonry **fireplace** was the central **structural** element of the original house

**Brick** piers replaced stone **foundations** as houses began to settle into the soft ground

# The shotgun was shaped by the need for worker housing

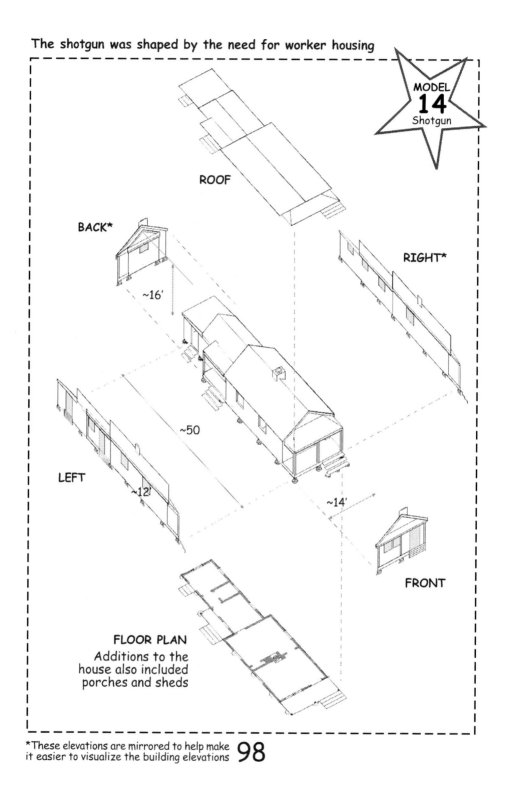

MODEL
**14**
Shotgun

ROOF

BACK*

RIGHT*

~16'

~50

LEFT

~12'

~14'

FRONT

FLOOR PLAN
Additions to the
house also included
porches and sheds

**Bungalows were an alternative to high density housing**

These **small** houses offered relatively peaceful and quiet **neighborhoods** for homeowners who could afford to **escape** the congestion and density of the city.

Late 1800s-Early 1900s

STYLIZED FEATURES ON SMALL HOUSES INCREASED THEIR VALUE

The gently sloping **hip roofs** were covered with wood or asphalt **shingles**

The houses added **modern** conveniences like indoor **plumbing**, central heat, and **electricity**.

The **bungalow style** evolved into the **craftsman** movement in residential **design***

Full **basements** held the heating equipment as well as **storage** space accessible from **inside** the house

New **technologies**, ornamental **landscaping**, and decorative architectural **details** hinted at the expanding ideal of the **American dream**

*Bungalows were originally adapted from the peasant dwellings in Bengal, India

**The bungalow fulfilled the dream of home ownership**

Small houses built with **style**, convenience and plumbing and heating helped people **take pride** in the ownership of a new class of **production** homes.

*See "American Bungalow: 1880 to 1930," by Clay Lancaster

# The bungalow was practical and affordable

The kitchen, bedrooms, and bath **circled** a central living room

**Clean** and odorless plumbing allowed the **bathroom** to "move in" as a **sales** feature of the house

**Open** living and dining **rooms** created a comfortable and **efficient** space for families

Porches remained an **important** feature of the bungalow **style***

STREET

*See especially the book "American Bungalow Style" by Robert Winter

101

**The bungalow's typical floor plan was efficient and practical**

*Blocks of ice for refrigeration were delivered regularly from ice plants

102

A sense of style was important to homebuyers

# Small houses grow to become a consumer product

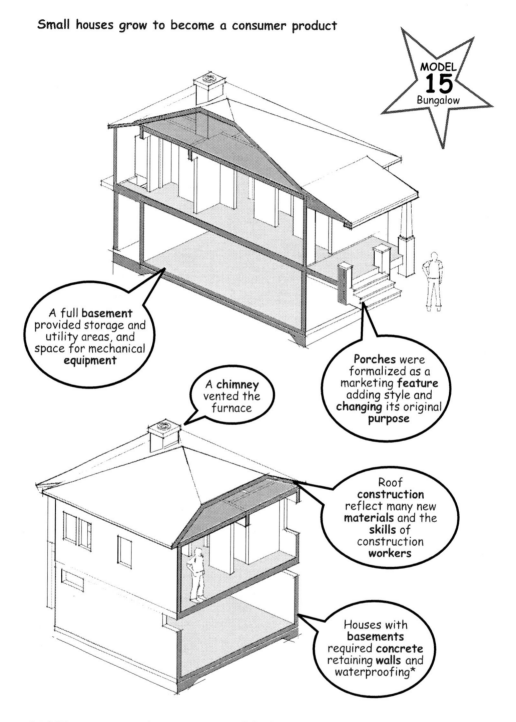

MODEL
**15**
Bungalow

A full **basement** provided storage and utility areas, and space for mechanical **equipment**

A **chimney** vented the furnace

**Porches** were formalized as a marketing **feature** adding style and **changing** its original **purpose**

Roof **construction** reflect many new **materials** and the **skills** of construction **workers**

Houses with **basements** required **concrete** retaining **walls** and waterproofing*

*A full basement required special equipment and reinforced masonry or concrete to build

# Bungalows were built as a housing product

**Builders** included style, craftsmanship, and modern conveniences as **sales** features that transformed **home building** into a competitive consumer **market**.

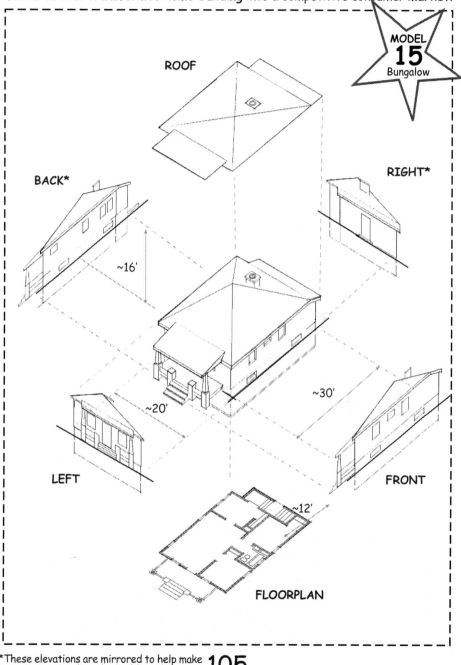

ROOF

MODEL
**15**
Bungalow

BACK*

RIGHT*

~16'

LEFT

~20'

~30'

FRONT

~12'

FLOORPLAN

Tract homes met the demand for affordable homeownership

Crowded cities and a **growing** middle class with automobiles and good roads and highways created a market for mass **produced** residential **developments.***

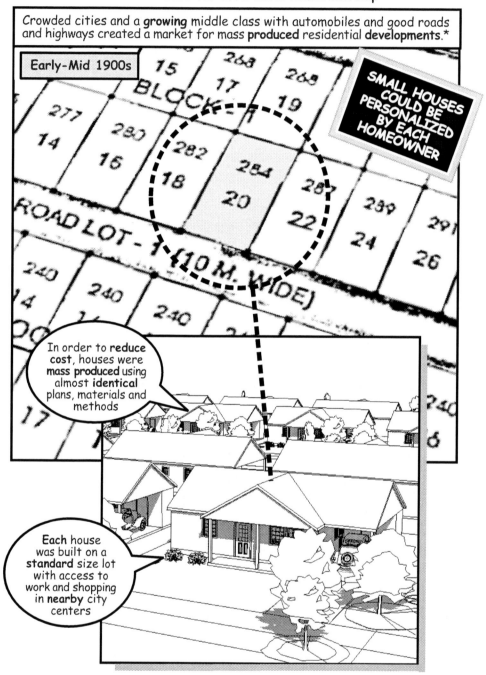

Early-Mid 1900s

SMALL HOUSES COULD BE PERSONALIZED BY EACH HOMEOWNER

In order to **reduce cost**, houses were **mass produced** using almost **identical** plans, materials and methods

Each house was built on a **standard** size lot with access to work and shopping in **nearby** city centers

*See "Entrepreneurial Vernacular: Subdivisions in the 1920s" by Carolyn Loeb

The automobile changed the shape of small houses

**These houses were built to be simple and affordable**

Production **houses** were built by the **same builder** to include conveniences that met the **needs** of a family living and working in an **expanding** economy.

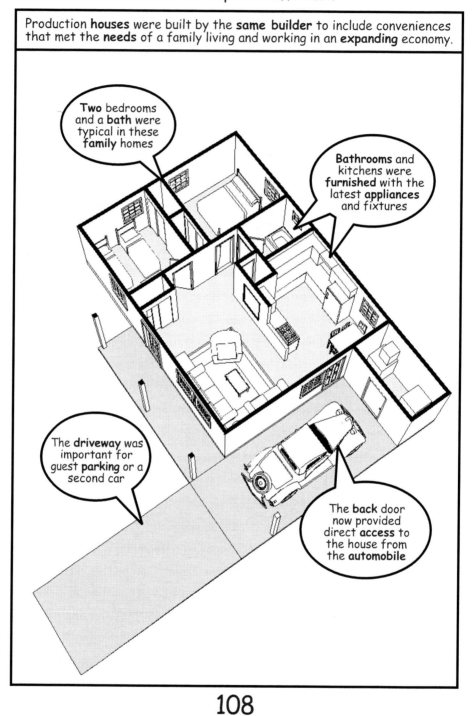

Storage **rooms** and **closets** for food, linens, clothing, appliances and other **consumer** products were necessary to store the family's growing **possessions***

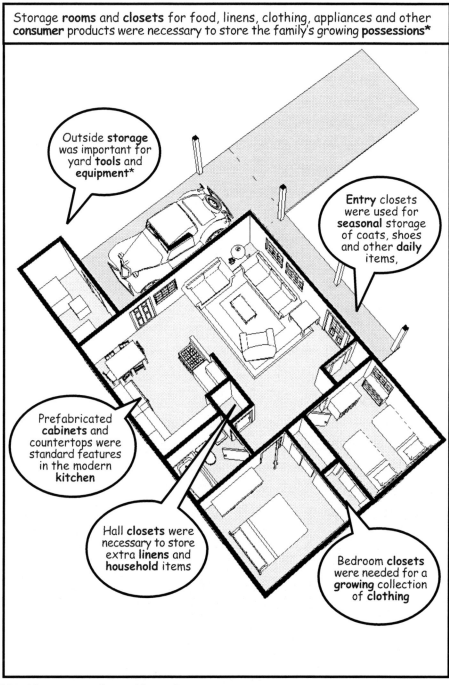

Outside **storage** was important for yard **tools** and **equipment***

**Entry** closets were used for **seasonal** storage of coats, shoes and other **daily** items,

Prefabricated **cabinets** and countertops were standard features in the modern **kitchen**

Hall **closets** were necessary to store extra **linens** and **household** items

Bedroom **closets** were needed for a **growing** collection of **clothing**

*Outside areas were also used for appliances like washing machines and clothes lines

Minimal decoration helped make the house affordable*

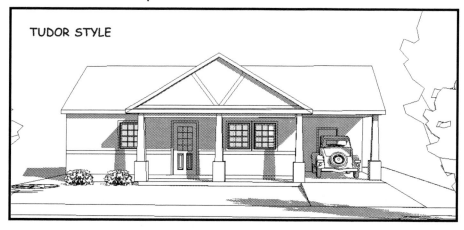

TUDOR STYLE

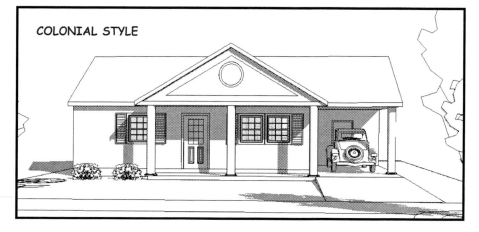

COLONIAL STYLE

RANCH STYLE

*The same plan was decorated with different stylistic features to appeal to home buyers

Wood framed buildings were easier to mass produce

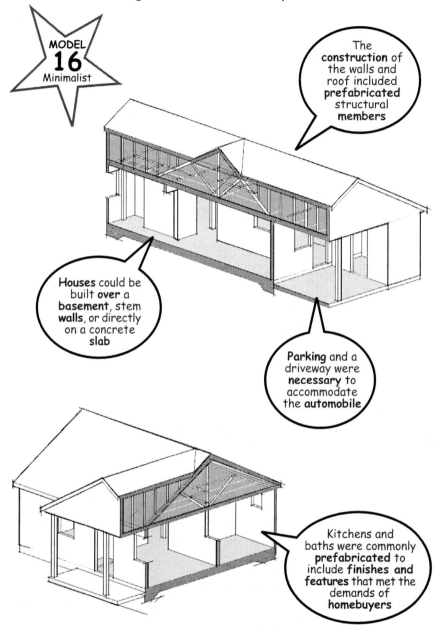

MODEL
**16**
Minimalist

The **construction** of the walls and roof included **prefabricated** structural **members**

**Houses** could be built **over** a **basement**, stem **walls**, or directly on a concrete **slab**

**Parking** and a driveway were **necessary** to accommodate the **automobile**

Kitchens and baths were commonly **prefabricated** to include **finishes and features** that met the demands of **homebuyers**

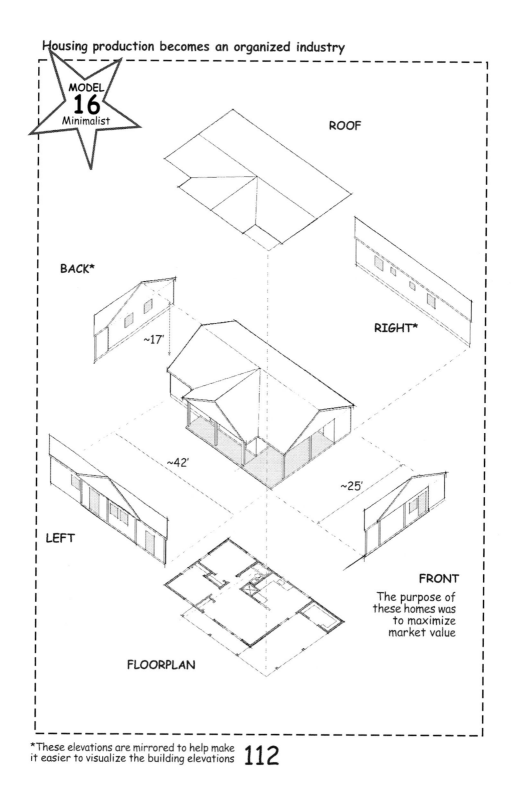

MODEL
**16**
Minimalist

ROOF

BACK*

RIGHT*

~17'

LEFT

~42'

~25'

FRONT

The purpose of
these homes was
to maximize
market value

FLOORPLAN

# CHAPTER SIX
## Super SMALL

For some, the freedom offered by open roads and an automobile made the idea of living in a secure home in the suburbs difficult to endure. Many took to the road in travel trailers and car campers either to escape their regulated lives for a few weeks or to find new lives wherever there was work.

### Moveable houses
Travel trailers took advantage of good roads and "tin can campgrounds" to set up temporary homes close to work or a vacation spot.* These camps were similar to the compounds of early settlers. Each trailer provided the basic needs and privacy necessary to make the gated community a home.

Trailers were also built to look more like little houses. These were moveable houses that could be placed on vacant land or in the backyard of a willing neighbor. A tiny house provided the same basic needs of a one room settler's cabin in the wilderness or on Walden Pond, but could be set up quickly or easily moved to another location if some new opportunity presented itself.

### Relocatable houses
Squatters build moveable houses without wheels to follow similar economic opportunities. These fragile little houses are often built on invaded land from materials that can be gathered from things that are found around them. The houses must remain small and simple with very few furnishings so they can be quickly deconstructed and moved if necessary.

The idea of a small and simple house that can be deconstructed and relocated whenever necessary hints at the potential of a tiny house built to be a completely self-contained home. In this house, the reduction of square footage adds focus and minimizes the demand for resources and energy.

*The "tin can" name came from the canned food travelers brought with them to eat

**Travel trailers provided shelter for a mobile society**

While some used **travel trailers** as homes to **settle** new areas, many **homeowners** used trailers as temporary **housing** on extended **vacations**.

Early-Mid 1900s

The **value** of a house also meant it could be **bought** and **sold** as homeowners **moved on** to new opportunities

**Contented** lives and **steady** work created a new **necessity** for a "much needed" **vacation**

**Travel** trailers **provided** all the conveniences of a **home** plus the mobility of the **open road**

### Tin can camps become destination communities

Travel trailers **filled** the need for **basic housing** in almost any place there was room to park. Tin can **tourist camps** were their own walled **community** complete with **security** gates, roads, play areas, water, and **communal** toilets and baths.

**Mobile houses provide simple and affordable housing**

These little **houses** were used for both **vacations** and worker **housing**

PRIVATE AND COMMUNITY SPACE JOIN TO MAKE A HOME

**Workers** lived in parts of the camp where **employers** could pick them up each morning

The **tiny house** filled the need for **mobility** and **flexibility** in a simple **shelter**

INDOOR (Private)

OUTDOOR (Community)

The **house** combined **indoor** and **outdoor** spaces to make a **home**

CAMP

For a view of tin can camp life "Indispensable Outcasts: Hobo Workers." Tobias Higbie.

## Efficiency and flexibility are built into a travel trailer

Early travel **trailers** worked well as a **tiny** house because both the furnishings and **living** spaces could accommodate a **variety** of **configurations**.

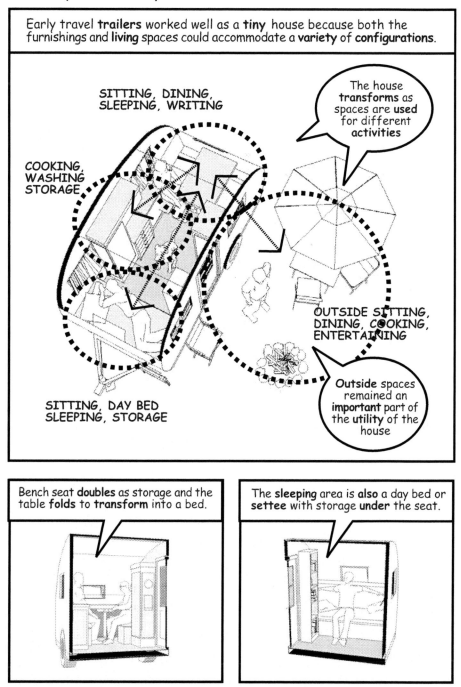

SITTING, DINING,
SLEEPING, WRITING

COOKING,
WASHING
STORAGE

The house **transforms** as spaces are **used** for different activities

SITTING, DAY BED
SLEEPING, STORAGE

OUTSIDE SITTING,
DINING, COOKING,
ENTERTAINING

Outside spaces remained an **important** part of the **utility** of the house

Bench seat **doubles** as storage and the table **folds** to **transform** into a bed.

The **sleeping** area is **also** a day bed or **settee** with storage **under** the seat.

For the evolution of the travel trailer see "Ready to Roll" by Doug Keister and others

**Functional and efficient design for compact living***

The entry **door** divided the **interior** into two activity **areas** that worked together as a **living** and **dining** room and **converted** to beds for **sleeping**.

A **table** top **lowers** to the bench level to form a **double** bed

Built in shelving and **cabinets** for storage

The day **bed** could be used for **sitting** sleeping and **storage**

TOWING TONGUE

The kitchen and pantry were located on the wall **opposite** the entry door with **cabinets** over and under a **sink** and with a **stove** for cooking and **heating**.

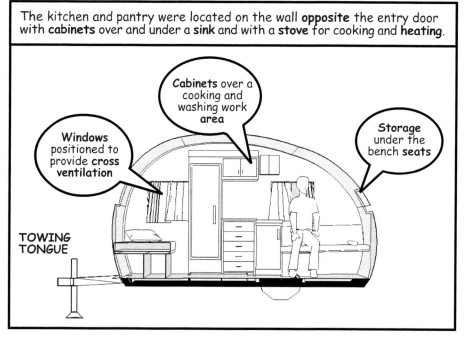

Windows positioned to provide **cross ventilation**

Cabinets over a cooking and washing work area

Storage under the bench **seats**

TOWING TONGUE

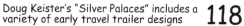

Doug Keister's "Silver Palaces" includes a variety of early travel trailer designs **118**

## The furnishings and activities had to be balanced

The tiny house was built with a **minimum** of **materials** and balanced on a **steel** frame to **distribute** the weight of the house **equally** over the wheels and tongue.

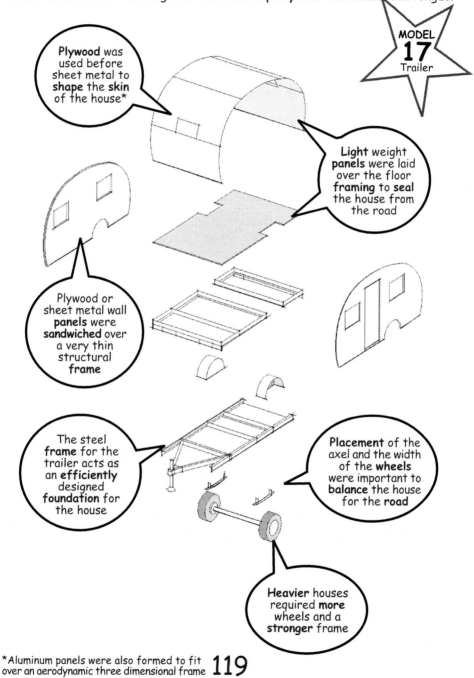

**Plywood** was used before sheet metal to **shape** the **skin** of the house*

MODEL
**17**
Trailer

**Light** weight **panels** were laid over the floor **framing** to **seal** the house from the road

Plywood or sheet metal wall **panels** were **sandwiched** over a very thin structural **frame**

The steel **frame** for the trailer acts as an **efficiently** designed **foundation** for the house

**Placement** of the axel and the width of the **wheels** were important to **balance** the house for the **road**

**Heavier** houses required **more** wheels and a **stronger** frame

*Aluminum panels were also formed to fit over an aerodynamic three dimensional frame

119

## These little houses were built for mobility

The design and **construction** of the travel trailer had to structurally balance the interior **activities** within the fixed floor plan. The **built-in** cabinets and furnishings were necessary to make the space **function** as a **one room** house.

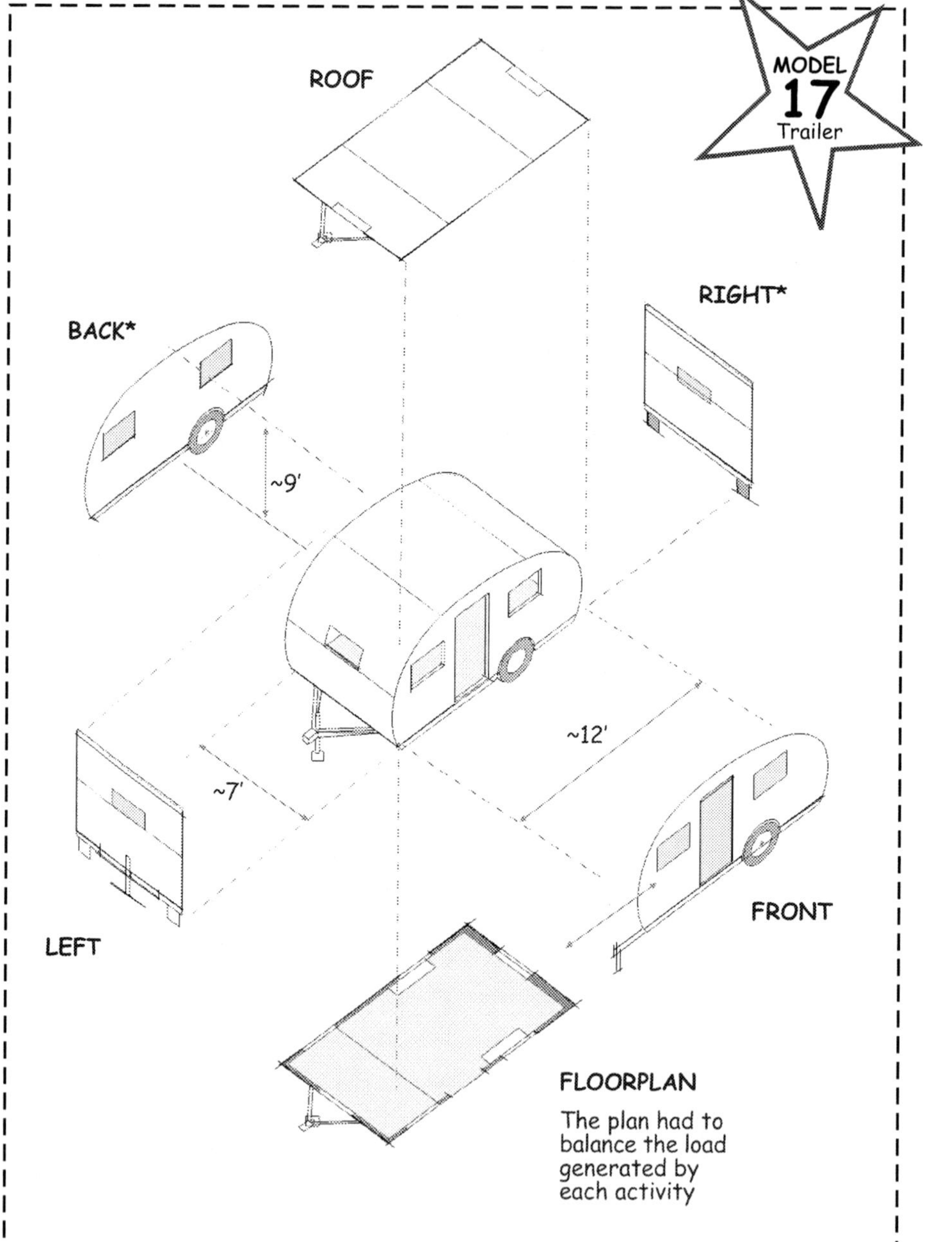

ROOF

MODEL
**17**
Trailer

RIGHT*

BACK*

~9'

~12'

~7'

FRONT

LEFT

FLOORPLAN

The plan had to
balance the load
generated by
each activity

Life on the edge of society in a movable house

Mid-Late 1900s

TINY HOUSES REDUCE THEIR ENVIRONMENTAL AND SOCIAL PRESENCE

COMMUNITY SPACE

Access to the city for **work** and other **services** is important to **survival**

A moveable house **avoids** many of the **regulations** necessary with a permanent structure

For many, **mobility** means living in a car or shopping cart, for others its a tiny house on **wheels***

PRIVATE SPACE

*This tiny house was built by Jay Shaffer.
See www.tumbleweedhouses.com

**A tiny house offers very affordable housing**

This tiny house was **manufactured** off site and moved onto land in an **existing** neighborhood with a **minimal** impact on either city services or quality of life.

Because the **house** is on **wheels** it was set up quickly and **blended** into the backyard

The **tiny** house provides an **affordable** home in what looks like a garden shed

Once moved onto the land, the **scale** and exterior **features** of the house meant it could be **landscaped** to make it almost **invisible** to neighbors.

The house was **hooked up** to basic services by a **garden hose** and an extension cord

The house's **wheels** were **covered** to make it less visible

## Wood construction makes a trailer look like a house

Conventional design and **common** construction materials are built onto a steel trailer frame to **make** the tiny house **look** and feel like a comfortable home.*

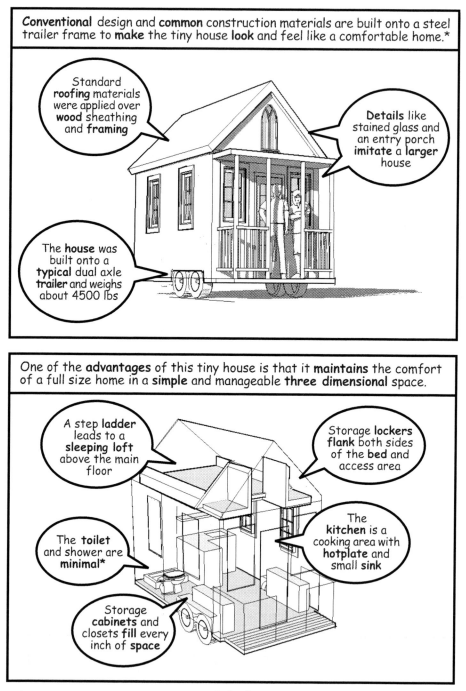

Standard **roofing** materials were applied over **wood** sheathing and **framing**

Details like stained glass and an entry porch **imitate** a **larger** house

The **house** was built onto a **typical** dual axle **trailer** and weighs about 4500 lbs

One of the **advantages** of this tiny house is that it **maintains** the comfort of a full size home in a **simple** and manageable **three dimensional** space.

A step **ladder** leads to a **sleeping loft** above the main floor

Storage **lockers flank** both sides of the **bed** and access area

The **toilet** and shower are **minimal**\*

The **kitchen** is a cooking area with **hotplate** and small **sink**

Storage **cabinets** and closets **fill** every inch of **space**

*The compact bathroom in this house is combination shower, sink, and water closet

**A small and simple space means a small and simple life**

The **interior** layout of a tiny house was able to **meet the needs** of its owners because it was **built** to be used **for** clearly defined needs and **purposes**.

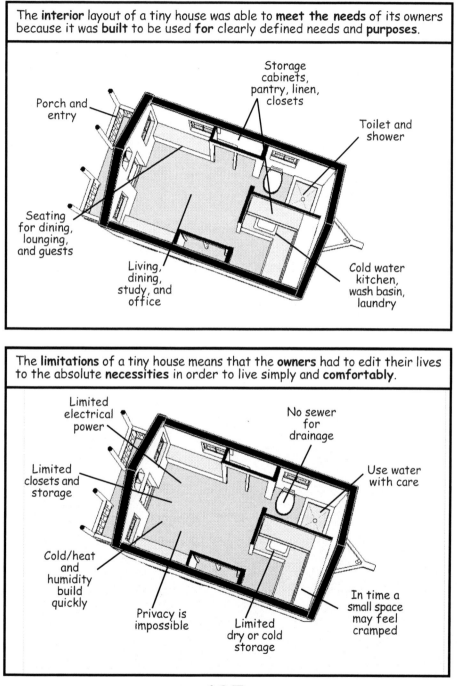

Porch and entry

Storage cabinets, pantry, linen, closets

Toilet and shower

Seating for dining, lounging, and guests

Living, dining, study, and office

Cold water kitchen, wash basin, laundry

The **limitations** of a tiny house means that the **owners** had to edit their lives to the absolute **necessities** in order to live simply and **comfortably**.

Limited electrical power

No sewer for drainage

Limited closets and storage

Use water with care

Cold/heat and humidity build quickly

Privacy is impossible

Limited dry or cold storage

In time a small space may feel cramped

Built with standard wood frame construction materials*

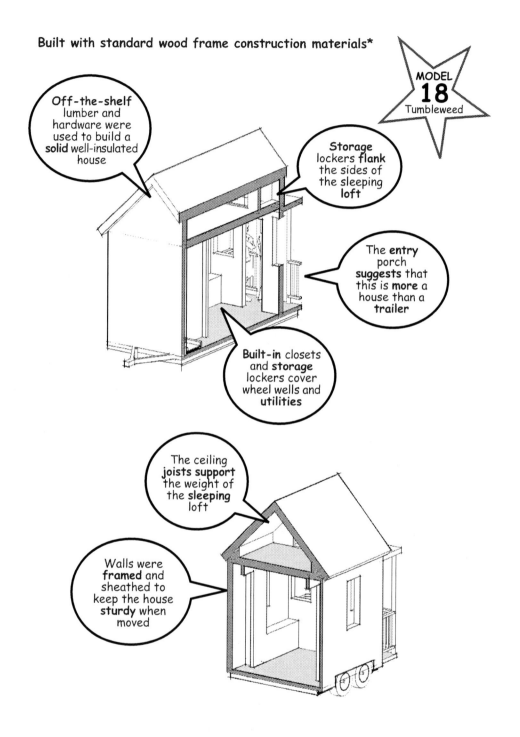

MODEL
**18**
Tumbleweed

Off-the-shelf lumber and hardware were used to build a **solid** well-insulated house

**Storage** lockers **flank** the sides of the sleeping **loft**

The **entry** porch **suggests** that this is **more** a house than a **trailer**

**Built-in** closets and **storage** lockers cover wheel wells and **utilities**

The ceiling **joists support** the weight of the **sleeping** loft

Walls were **framed** and sheathed to keep the house **sturdy** when moved

This moveable house is flexible and sustainable

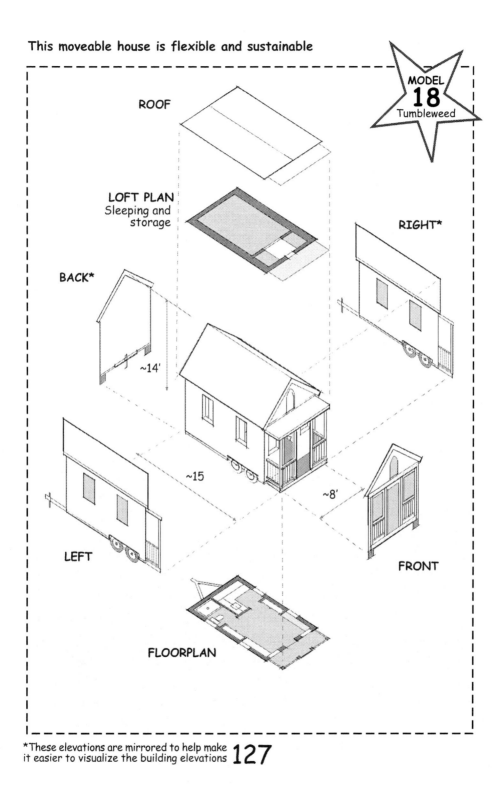

MODEL
**18**
Tumbleweed

ROOF

LOFT PLAN
Sleeping and
storage

RIGHT*

BACK*

~14'

~15

~8'

LEFT

FRONT

FLOORPLAN

A deconstructible house without wheels

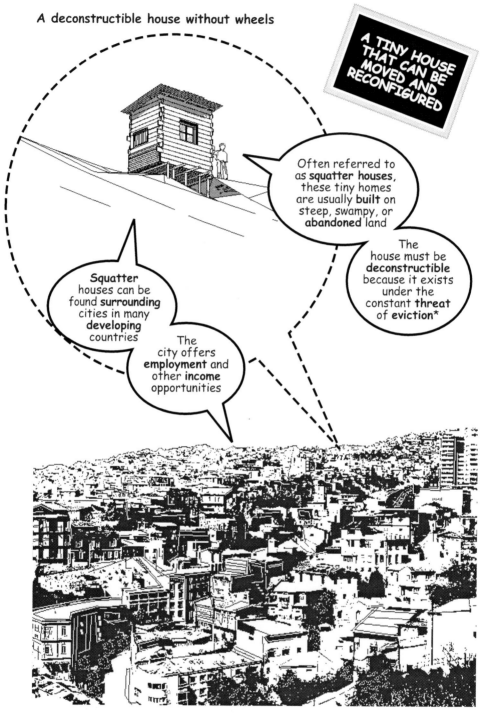

A TINY HOUSE THAT CAN BE MOVED AND RECONFIGURED

Often referred to as **squatter houses**, these tiny homes are usually **built** on steep, swampy, or **abandoned** land

The house must be **deconstructible** because it exists under the constant **threat of eviction***

**Squatter** houses can be found **surrounding** cities in many **developing** countries

The city offers **employment** and other **income** opportunities

*See especially "The Other Path" by Hernando de Soto

128

**The house was designed and bulit by its owners***

When **affordable housing** is not available, **squatter houses** like this one provide economical relocatable **homes** for their owners. The tiny house meets the **unique needs** of the hundreds of thousands of **families** that live in them.

1985-1990s

Recycled construction **materials** were gathered from local sources**

The house **was built** so that it could be quickly **deconstructed** and moved

**Hinged** hatch provides **ventilation** and an emergency **exit**

Foundation and framing **design** is intuitive and **fragile** in a wind

## Small, simple and sustainable

The **tiny house** would not be possible without the **collective efforts** of family and friends. As the **owners** gained confidence that they would not be evicted, the **house evolved** and **grew** as new tools or materials were found and **added**.

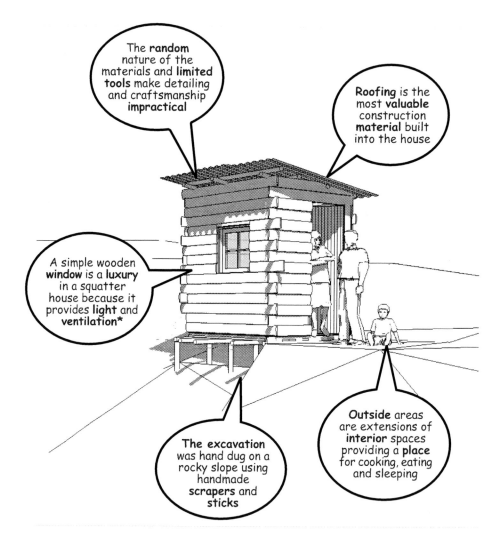

The **random** nature of the materials and **limited tools** make detailing and craftsmanship **impractical**

**Roofing** is the most **valuable** construction **material** built into the house

A simple wooden **window** is a **luxury** in a squatter house because it provides **light** and **ventilation***

The excavation was hand dug on a rocky slope using handmade **scrapers** and sticks

**Outside** areas are extensions of **interior** spaces providing a **place** for cooking, eating and sleeping

## Living spaces are multifunctional and efficient

Since **nothing is wasted** and everything has value, materials are **added** as they are discovered, making the house a **useable** form of three dimensional **storage.**\*

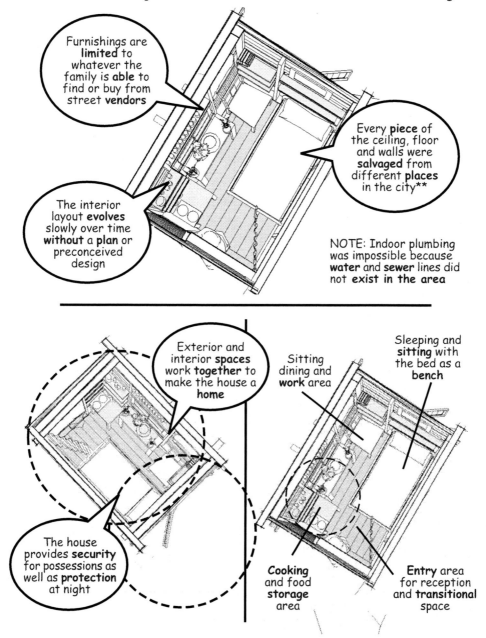

Furnishings are **limited** to whatever the family is **able** to find or buy from street **vendors**

The interior layout **evolves** slowly over time **without** a **plan** or preconceived design

Every **piece** of the ceiling, floor and walls were **salvaged** from different **places** in the city\*\*

NOTE: Indoor plumbing was impossible because **water** and **sewer** lines did not **exist in the area**

Exterior and interior **spaces** work **together** to make the house a **home**

The house provides **security** for possessions as well as **protection** at night

Sitting dining and **work** area

Sleeping and **sitting** with the bed as a **bench**

**Cooking** and food **storage** area

**Entry** area for reception and **transitional** space

\*Even discarded nails and scraps have value and find a place somewhere in the house

\*\*With little money, materials were found in the trash, gutters, or traded for labor

The construction process was the land invasion*

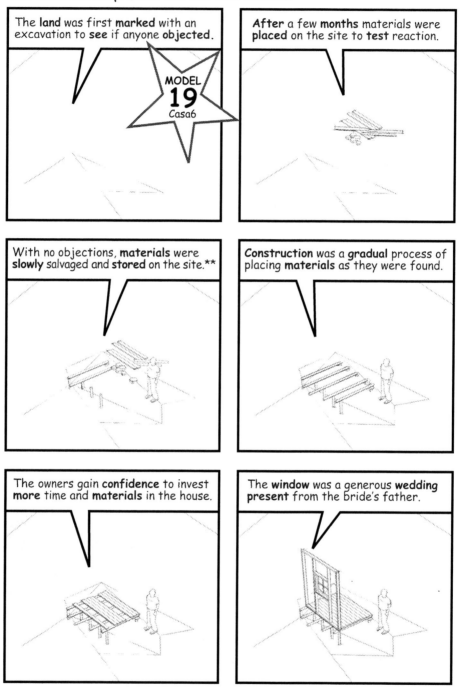

The **land** was first **marked** with an excavation to **see** if anyone **objected**.

MODEL
**19**
Casa6

After a few **months** materials were **placed** on the site to **test** reaction.

With no objections, **materials** were **slowly** salvaged and **stored** on the site.**

**Construction** was a **gradual** process of placing **materials** as they were found.

The owners gain **confidence** to invest **more** time and **materials** in the house.

The **window** was a generous **wedding present** from the bride's father.

*The process was documented in "Social Production of Architecture" Dennis Fukai

132

**If materials were not stolen or destroyed it suggested the invasion might be successful

## The house grew as cautious owners invested more resources

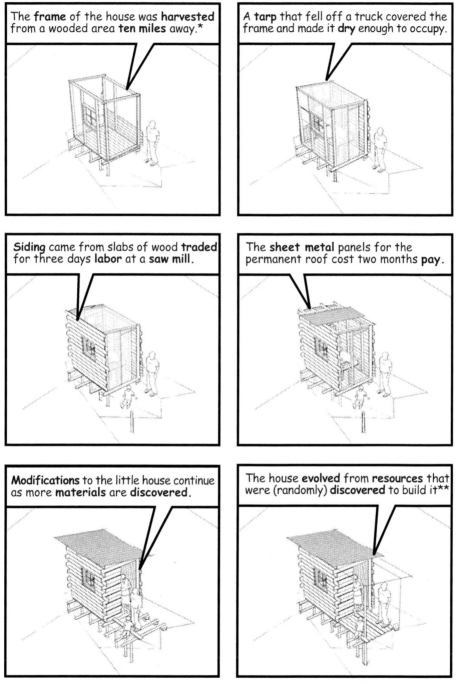

The **frame** of the house was **harvested** from a wooded area **ten miles** away.*

A **tarp** that fell off a truck covered the frame and made it **dry** enough to occupy.

**Siding** came from slabs of wood **traded** for three days **labor** at a **saw mill**.

The **sheet metal** panels for the permanent roof cost two months **pay**.

**Modifications** to the little house continue as more **materials** are **discovered**.

The house **evolved** from **resources** that were (randomly) **discovered** to build it**

*These materials had to be hand carried to the construction site by the family

**133**

**This tiny house evolved over seven years of invasion and slow construction

### The house is deconstructable, reconfigurable, and relocatable

Every **piece** of the little house is part of a **collection** of materials that have been gathered over its **years** of construction. A major discovery like a wood beam would mean a complete redesign, **deconstruction**, and reconfiguration.

*Any trimming or fitting actually wastes material and limits the potential of its reuse

**Stones and tires were used as balast to hold down the sheet metal roofing

## This house was built to be continually changed

The door and windows and the floor and wall boards are **loosely** fastened to the **frame** so they can be **deconstructed** and **reused** in another configuration.

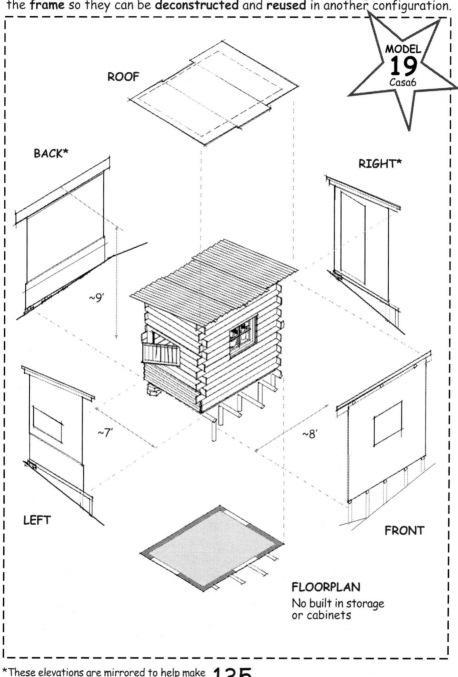

ROOF

MODEL
**19**
Casa6

BACK*

RIGHT*

~9'

LEFT

~7'

~8'

FRONT

FLOORPLAN
No built in storage
or cabinets

**A deconstructible house that is simple to build**

Early 2000s

ENVIRONMENTAL TECHNOLOGIES INCREASE SUSTAINABILITY

The **scale** of a tiny house **means** it requires **less material**

It also **means** that the house can be **located** in difficult or **remote** locations

The **purpose** of this tiny house was to **test** the potential of **sustainability**

Built like a **squatter's** house, the house was erected, then **deconstructed** and **moved**

## Engineered for survival and sanctuary

This tiny house was built to **test** the environmental **loads** imposed by both the **weather** and **occupants** of the structure over a period of **14 months**.

Solar panels for **power** for lights, radio, and a laptop **computer***

Gable **panels** with **insulated** walls and a **clerestory** add light to the loft

**Panelized** walls included door, window, and **storage** alcoves that **increased** the living **area** and provided basic **conveniences** like plumbing, heat, and power.

Insulated roof and skylight **panels** for light and **ventilation**

Battery pack**

Water and **power** systems

*Solar panels provide limited power and must be carefully balanced with demand

137

*Batteries contain toxic materials and must be vented and regularly serviced

Sustainable living in a small and simple tiny house

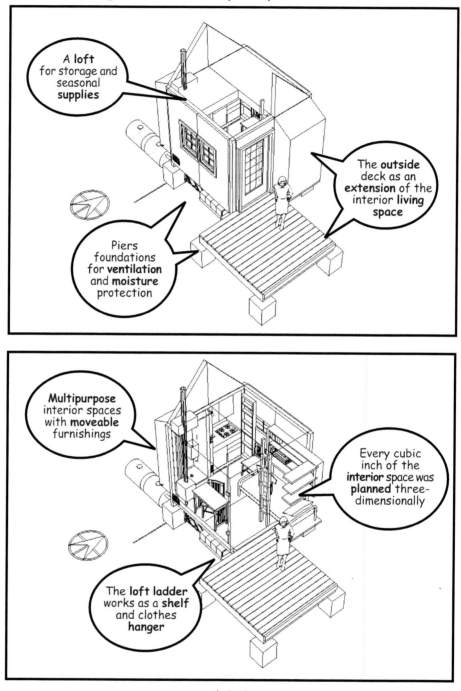

# Environmental technologies provide modern conveniences

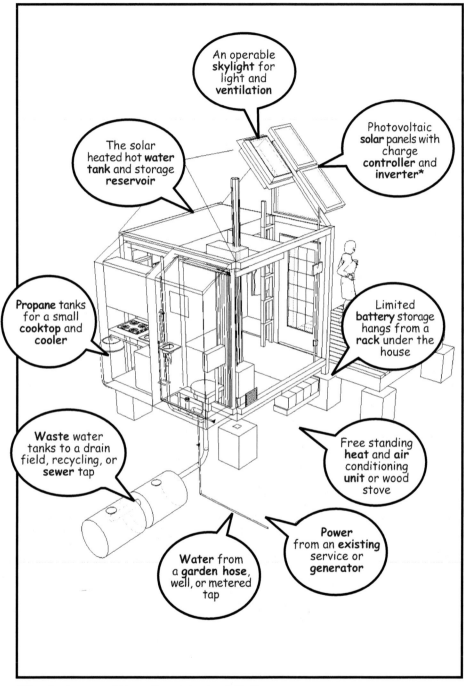

An operable **skylight** for light and **ventilation**

Photovoltaic **solar** panels with charge **controller** and **inverter**\*

The solar heated hot **water tank** and storage **reservoir**

**Propane** tanks for a small **cooktop** and **cooler**

Limited **battery** storage hangs from a **rack** under the house

**Waste** water tanks to a drain field, recycling, or **sewer** tap

Free standing **heat** and **air** conditioning **unit** or wood stove

**Water** from a **garden hose**, well, or metered tap

**Power** from an **existing** service or **generator**

## Deconstructable like a squatter's home

Wall panels **snap** onto a **structural frame** for assembly and **deconstruction**. The house could then be moved and reconfigured for construction in **another location**.

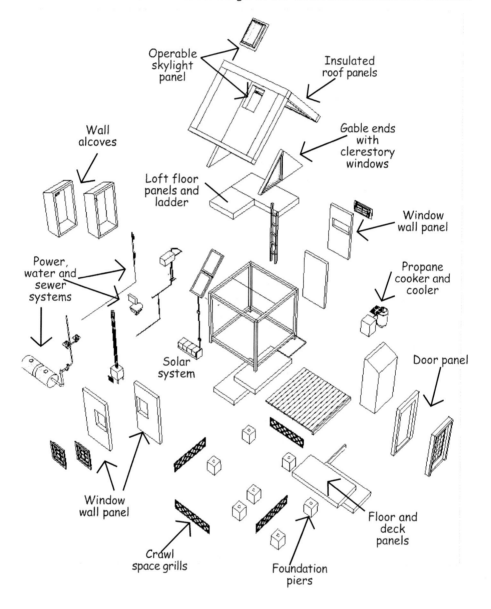

Operable skylight panel

Insulated roof panels

Wall alcoves

Gable ends with clerestory windows

Loft floor panels and ladder

Window wall panel

Power, water and sewer systems

Propane cooker and cooler

Solar system

Door panel

Window wall panel

Floor and deck panels

Crawl space grills

Foundation piers

**The house was built slowly piece by piece**

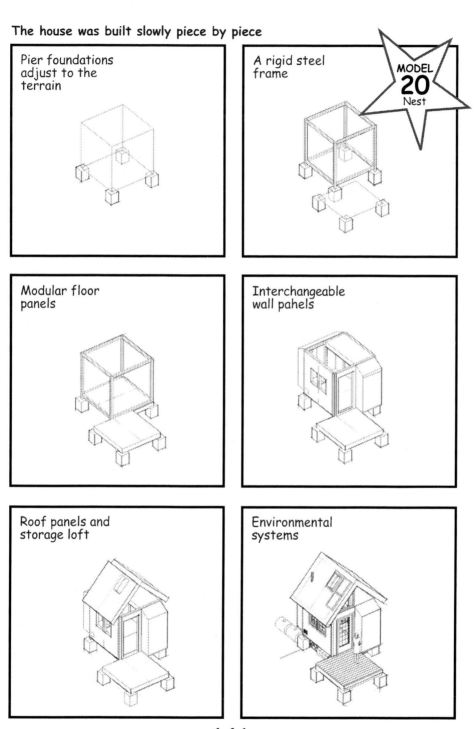

Pier foundations adjust to the terrain

A rigid steel frame

MODEL
**20**
Nest

Modular floor panels

Interchangeable wall pahels

Roof panels and storage loft

Environmental systems

**Reuseable pieces built to be reconfigured and expanded**

Like a squatter's house, this **tiny house** was built to be **deconstructed** and **reconfigured** with a minimal loss of **materials** as new technologies are found.

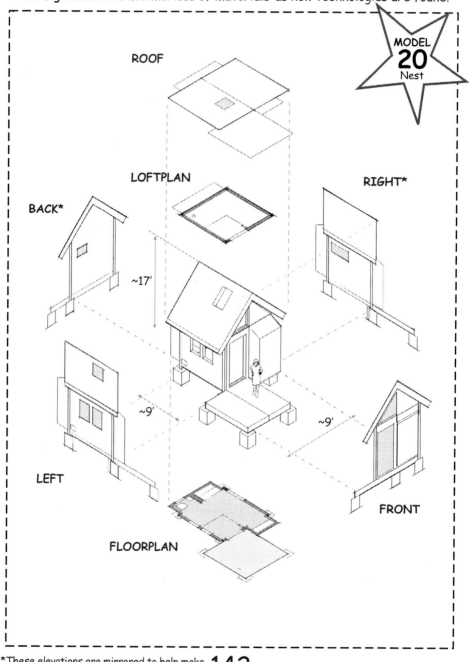

ROOF

MODEL
**20**
Nest

LOFTPLAN

BACK*

RIGHT*

~17'

~9'

~9'

LEFT

FRONT

FLOORPLAN

# CHAPTER SEVEN
## 3D MODELS ON THE CD

## A SUMMARY OF THINGS TO THINK ABOUT IN 3D

**Mass produced houses are built to sell**

The 3D models for the McMansions are simple massing models* showing the size and scale of two popular houses built by a leading residential developer in the USA. The houses were built for different market targets and are included in the book to set the stage for thinking about small houses.

The McMansion models show how floor plans are extruded into houses with the flat ceilings and segregated rooms common to mass produced housing. The spaces that result are FLAT and two dimensional. They also consume resources for the sake of mass market appeal.

In the models you can see how much of the roof of a McMansion is wasted in unusable attics. Large roofs are added to improve the look of the house from the street. Curb appeal is important to marketing, but considering the resources used to fill the volume of these attics, a lot of material is wasted in order to make a sale. It's also important to consider the lost potential of this space for the homeowner.

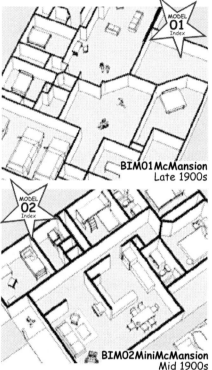

BIM01McMansion
Late 1900s

BIM02MiniMcMansion
Mid 1900s

**Small houses are built purposefully with clearly defined functions**

The massing models for the granny and family houses were included to help visualize the interior of two houses that were built purposefully with clearly defined functions in mind. The interiors of these houses are open to upper floors, clerestories, or storage lofts. Unlike two-dimensional houses with extruded floor plans, the volume of these open spaces add to the visual potential of a small house.

*A massing model is built to be a simplified study of 3D shape, orientation, and space.

The 3D model for the granny unit shows how sight lines can be built into the interior to allow occupants to "feel" the volume of a larger room. The purpose of this house is to provide a stimulating space as an alternative to an institutionalized assisted living facility. You can see in this model how the open feel adds to the experience of living in a purposeful space.

BIM03Granny
2004

The 3D model for the family house is a good example of how a home can be built purposefully to support the activities of a family. The small house fits the family like a glove because it serves their clearly defined needs. Rooms are joined to create an open plan and multipurpose areas for family activities. This results in longer view planes and the full feel of the total volume of the space.

BIM04Family
2003

**Small houses include the community that surrounded them**

Early settlement houses began as walled enclosures that protected the people living inside the compound. As the walls of the enclosure were strengthened, the settlers built little houses to replace family campsites. The walled enclosure offered security and the small houses provided privacy and personal space.

Important is that people lived and worked in both the private and community space. The purpose of the house was therefore to define this sense of shared space. The 3D model shows how the houses provided a separation from the community in which it was constructed. Even though the buildings were almost exactly the same, these small houses provided families with private areas for cooking, sleeping, and sitting together in bad weather. Activities outside of the house were communal and social.

BIM05Settlement
Early1600s

**Small houses blend interior and exterior working spaces**

Settler houses were built by pioneers who moved onto land that needed to be cleared and worked before it could support a family. The house began as a covered campsite for basic shelter. Over time, the shelter was replaced by a simple one room house using materials found on or near the home site. As the land became more productive, the house might be expanded or abandoned depending on the settler's success on the homestead, but its purpose remained to provide enough shelter to help settlers work the land.

The 3D massing model for this settler's house shows how the porch and yard worked together with the interior of the house. The porch provided a shaded area immediately adjacent to the indoor living area to work. Outside spaces increased the utility and function of the inside of the house by extending activity areas beyond the walls of the single room.

**BIM06Settlers**
Early 1600-Late 1700s

### Crackers begin to standardize small house construction

The purpose of a cracker's house was to comfortably support a family working the land. Crackers settled land close to roads, railroads, or waterways that could provide access to markets for products harvested from their land. These routes were also used to bring in construction materials to build their houses. Access to these materials helped the crackers build more reliable and comfortable houses.

**BIM07Cracker**
The 1800s

The massing model for the cracker house shows how the vernacular style of these houses was replicated by many of these settlers. For a cracker, the main house often began with a wagon full of supplies and a few skilled workers. The more materials they could afford, the bigger the house would become. Most important, the shape and form of the house could be carefully planned by their builders and tailored to the needs of the inhabitants.

### Small houses and their settings were sources of inspiration

Henry David Thoreau built a small house as a way to rethink the necessities of his crowded life. He chose a quiet spot not far from a growing town where his family owned a pencil factory. The site he chose was on a friend's property next to a pond. With this site in mind, Thoreau set about building the simplest house that he could imagine.

The 3D massing model shows that the result was almost identical to a settler's house. Like them, he oriented the house to take advantage of his site and the resources that surrounded it. For Thoreau, placement on the site was as important as the simplicity of the house itself. The purpose of the site and the house was to provide shelter from society and the environment so that he could focus on the daily tasks of living small. For Thoreau, these tasks gave him time to think deeply about his place in his surroundings. He returned to the city after two years with a book that would begin the modern environmental movement.

**BIM08Thoreau**
Mid1800s

145

### Access to the work added function and purpose

Farmhouses grew as additions to the original house were built to accommodate the activities of the farm and family. The added rooms reflect the availability of furnishings and materials as well as the increasing confidence settlers had about markets for their products.

**BIM09Farmhouses**
Mid-Late 1800s

The massing model for this farmhouse shows how new rooms continued to support the activities of the farm. Every part of the house was built for a specific purpose. This included sleeping rooms, kitchens, and living areas. Each room had an exterior door so workers could come and go without walking through the house. These doors reduced the need for hallways and gave immediate access to the activities of the farm.

### Small houses added to the protection of the natural environment

For a ranch house to be successful, a settler had to intuitively understand where to plant their fields, graze their live stock, and build the house. In fact, the site for the house and barn were critical to the success of a farm or ranch.

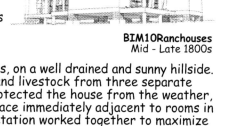

**BIM10Ranchouses**
Mid - Late 1800s

The 3D model for this ranch house shows how one family built their home with a clear understanding of its function and purpose as the center of the ranching activities. The house was sited near trees, on a well drained and sunny hillside. The family looked out at their gardens and livestock from three separate porches. While the trees shaded and protected the house from the weather, the porches provided sheltered living space immediately adjacent to rooms in the house. The porches and natural vegetation worked together to maximize the utility of the house.

### Small houses filled the need for basic worker housing

As farming and ranching expanded, worker housing became increasingly important. Small worker houses were built in clusters or villages a short distance from the farm. They remained simple and functional, but were different because their purpose moved away from a natural setting and farm activities toward the need to provide basic affordable housing.

**BIM11Worker**
Late 1800-Early1900s

The model for one of these houses illustrates the growing distance between the house and the land. The house is an efficient rectangle with a kitchen, dining, living area, and separate bedrooms.

146

Except for the addition of a bathroom or expanded kitchen, these houses were compact and efficient units built to provide basic comforts with a small entry porch, front and rear doors, and space for personal storage.

### Small house construction helped standardize methods and materials

The purpose of worker housing in company camps and towns was to provide employees and their families with a place to live close to work. In most cases, these houses were absolute minimal structures, providing only the basic necessities for their workers. They were built by contractors using organized labor, specialized trades, and coordinated material supplies.

**BIM12Company**
Late 1800s - Early 1900s

The massing model for a house built in one of these company towns shows how specialized labor worked systematically with standard materials to find new ways to mass produce housing. The purpose of this house was to provide the bare necessities of the workers with the least possible expense to the company. The production methods developed to meet that purpose helped spawn an industry of home builders.

### Townhouses could not adapt to changing needs

Developers built high density housing for the growing number of workers in the towns and cities of the USA. Because building sites close to the center of economic activity were scarce or expensive, townhouses were purposefully built on city lots to maximize the use of the land. These dense building sites and the townhouses that resulted required special skill to build and maintain.

The 3D massing model for one of the townhouses built during this time illustrates how compact these houses and their neighborhoods were for the people who lived in them. Small rooms were separated vertically by floors and stairways with access limited to a door on the ground floor. The townhouse fulfilled its initial purpose as a comfortable home, but they were difficult to modify

**BIM13Townhouses**
Mid 1800s

as the needs of a family changed. This inflexibility quickly led to overcrowded and oppressive living conditions.

### Small houses must be able to change and adapt over time

Shotguns were built on the outskirts of southern towns and cities in the USA to fill the need for worker housing. They were built in rows along the streets of city blocks on very narrow pieces of land. The narrow lots increased the efficiency of city services because more houses could be served on the street side of each block. This result was a line of identical but affordable houses.

## 147

The massing model for one of these houses shows how need and imagination joined to shape one of hundreds of variations of the shotgun house. Lots were often combined and houses were transformed as the original house evolved over time. Change and repurposing was important to the success of the shotgun. Even on a single narrow lot the original house could remain a simple one or two room shelter, expand to the back of the lot, add a second story, or be modified with a side hall to become a rooming house or apartment.

**BIM14Shotgun**
Late1800s

**Stylized features and details on small houses increased their value.**

The bungalow is an early example of how small houses were becoming stylized products for a growing middle class. They were built to appeal to an emerging need for housing in quiet neighborhoods outside the city center. These houses featured the craftsmanship and conveniences of comfortable bungalow living. They were set back on larger lots and easy for owners to personalize with landscaping and architectural details.

**BIM15Bungalow**
Late1800s-Early 1900s

The 3D model for the California bungalow on this CD is typical of houses built in almost every town and city in the USA. The massing model shows deep overhangs, low sloping roofs, basements, and attic rooms. The interior of the house included features like reliable plumbing, kitchen cabinets, appliances and central heating. The needs of the family were growing with the income of homeowners and the purpose of a small house was beginning to mirror the prosperity of a new breed of home buyers.

**Small houses were personalized with landscaping, decoration, and a car**

Tract houses were mass produced to meet the growing demand for housing outside the older neighborhoods of the USA. They were built with materials and methods that reflected the market strategies of home builders. As such, the house might include some stylistic decoration, but their purpose was affordable homeownership. This left owners with a blank slate to begin improving and personalizing their homes.

The 3D model for the tract house on the CD helps viewers visualize the appeal of these simple decorated boxes. They were important not so much for their simplicity but because they filled the desire for affordable home ownership in new

**BIM16Minimalist**
Early-Mid 1900s

neighborhoods with yards, sidewalks, and a special place for the family car. The automobile was a driving factor in the development of suburban residential communities.

## Private and community space join to make a tiny house a home

Whether driven by the need to be close to work in another town or simply the desire to take a vacation, travel trailers and tourist camps offered a way of life that included many of the comforts of home. The campground provided the security found in the early walled settlements, while the travel trailer provided the privacy found in any simple shelter. The sense of community necessary to make either place a home grew from the combination of inside and outside space.

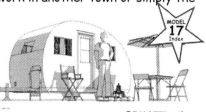

**BIM17Trailer**
Early-Mid 1900s

The 3D model of this travel trailer shows how it opened to the community that surrounded it. Living areas in front of the trailer were part of the campsite and open to interaction with neighbors and friends. The trailer itself squeezed the needs of a family into various combinations of usable space with storage compartments and furnishings built into every corner. The tiny house was able to change its configuration from dining to sleeping and visiting to working in two distinct areas on either side of its only door. But the travel trailer's success as a comfortable home came from the life that was shared beyond its walls.

## Tiny houses reduced their environmental and social presence

Variations on the original travel trailer included a variety of little houses built on wheels. This included a number of imaginative homes on truck frames and old buses by an increasingly mobile generation. These moveable houses bypassed the codes and ordinances that are often required of permanent structures because building codes do not normally regulate structures unless they are permanently installed on a site.

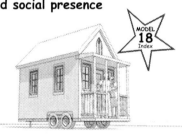

**BIM16Tumbleweed**
Mid-Late 1900s

The massing model for one of these moveable houses shows how the galley kitchen and toilet work with the living and eating area to create a tiny but comfortable multipurpose space. The loft-attic for the house is used for reading, sleeping, and storage. The purpose of this house was to provide an affordable home that could blend into its neighborhood environment and allow it to be parked unobtrusively in a backyard.

## Tiny houses built to be deconstructed and moved or reconfigured

Tiny moveable houses that blend into the background of visually chaotic environments can be found in the squatter settlements that have grown around many industrialized centers. Also referred to as informal dwellings, squatter houses are built where building codes are unclear or difficult to enforce.* The purpose of these tiny houses is to slowly invade a piece of land and occupy it for as long as possible.

*The squatter process is described in books on "informal settlements." See especially "The Other Path," by Hernando De Soto

149

The 3D model for the squatter house included on the CD shows how one squatter family used a very slow construction process to invade a steep hillside close to their family and work in the city. Like Thoreau's house on Walden Pond, the tiny house occupied land it did not own, the frame of the house was cut from local forests, and many of its materials were salvaged from other buildings.

BIM19Casa6
1985-1990s

The house is moveable because at any time it can be deconstructed and transported to another location. It can also be deconstructed and completely reconfigured as new materials are discovered to change its form.

**Environmental technologies can be used to improve sustainability**

Tiny houses have long been used as garden structures, pool cabanas, hunting or fishing sheds, and wilderness shelters. They provide simple and sustainable living spaces with minimal maintenance, materials, and a single room to heat, light, and ventilate. The model for one of these tiny houses shows how its construction explores a more purposeful approach to the potential of a tiny house as an environmentally sustainable structure.

BIM20Nest
Early 2000s

The house is deconstructible, with insulated floor and wall panels bolted to a steel frame. The steeply pitched insulated roof panels include a skylight with open ceilings and clerestory windows for air circulation. The tiny house also has a number of environmental technologies to support its kitchen, bathroom, and multipurpose sleeping and work areas. Important is that the small size of the house is a key factor in its sustainability.

**CHECKLIST: The life of a small house**

>Purposeful with simple needs
>Clearly defined activities and functions
>Self-determined owner-builders

>Sightlines and pathways
>High ceilings for light and air
>Simple three dimensional volumes
>Open multipurpose rooms

>Share space with a community
>Oriented to the environment
>Direct access to improve circulation
>Blend interior and exterior space

>Flexible furnishings and construction
>Organized labor and process
>Use standard sizes and materials
>Minimal and simple decoration

>Open to modification and change
> Changes follow new purpose and needs
>Land use considers future plans
>Slow methodical construction

>Mobile and deconstructible elements
>Deconstructible panelized assemblies
>Modern technologies for sustainability

# OTHER BOOKS THAT MIGHT BE OF INTEREST

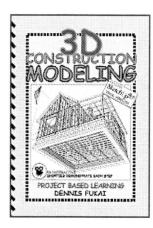

For those interested in building their own model this book starts from the ground up in a step by step approach to model construction

Covers construction graphics from a napkin sketch through a simple set of construction drawings. Includes 3D construction modeling

A step by step approach to designing, making, and maintaining a construction website including a homepage, project pages, and animations

---

## COMING SOON

**3D BIM MODELING:** Building information models in SketchUp
**BUILDING SIMPLE:** 3D Construction Documents for 4 small houses
**LIVING SUSTAINABLY:** A survey of simple environmental technologies

**I n s i t e b u i l d e r s**

16708 SW 132nd Lane
Archer FL 32618
http://insitebuilders.com

Email questions or comments to:
dennis@insitebuilders.com